HAVE A HAPPY HALLOWEEN!

01. DOT TO DOT

02. PIXEL COLOR

03. COLORING PAGES

04. DOTS LINES

Jennifer Rolling

Bright-Ideas Paper Publishing
Amazon.com/author/bright-ideas
Bright.IdeasPaperPublishing@gmail.com

Enjoy beautiful and relaxing with this easy coloring book from us.

Halloween is near. We've seen it written in the leaves falling from the trees – the witches are brewing up spooky times for all you hardworking students, and we're not just talking about the rain tapping on your window or the chimes going wild in the wind. We're talking Halloween activities you can enjoy with the family,

Why You Will Love this Book?

Relaxing Coloring Pages. Every page you color will pull you into a relaxing world where your responsibilities will seem to fade away...

Beautiful Illustrations. We've included unique images for you to express your creativity and make masterpieces. Which colors will you choose for this book?

Single-sided Pages. Every image is placed on its own black-backed page to reduce the bleed-through problem found in other coloring books.

Great for All Skill Levels. You can color every page however you want and there is no wrong way to color (even if you are a beginner).

Makes a Wonderful Gift. Know someone who loves to color? Make them smile by getting them a copy too. You could even color together!

NOTE:

Get creative! Don't worry so much about mistakes! We always provide printable copy of each page if you need. Send your requirements to us by email.

LET'S ENJOY!

THiS BOOK BeLONGS TO

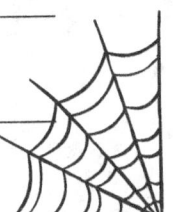

_____

_____

_____

COLORING TEST PAGE

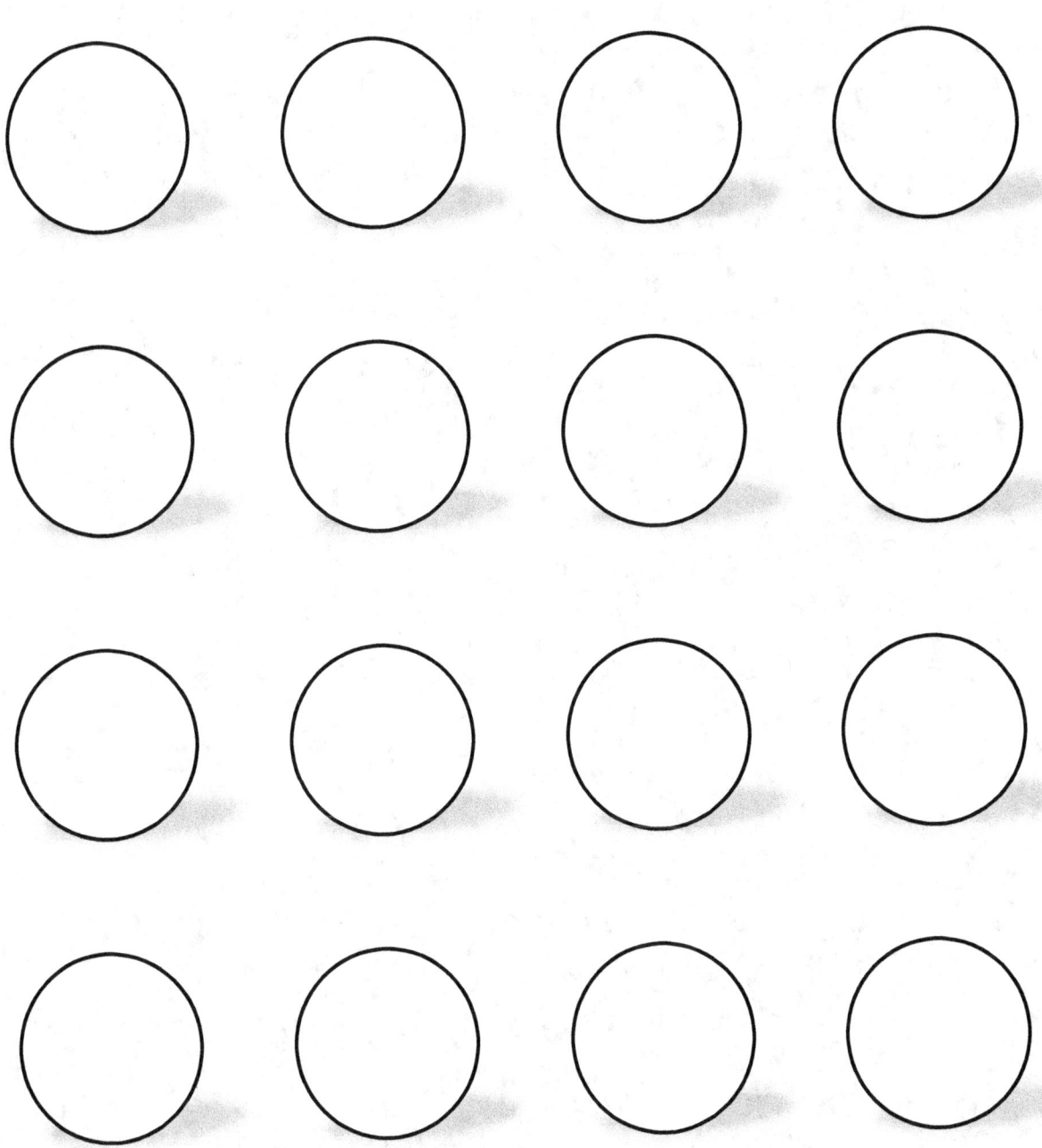

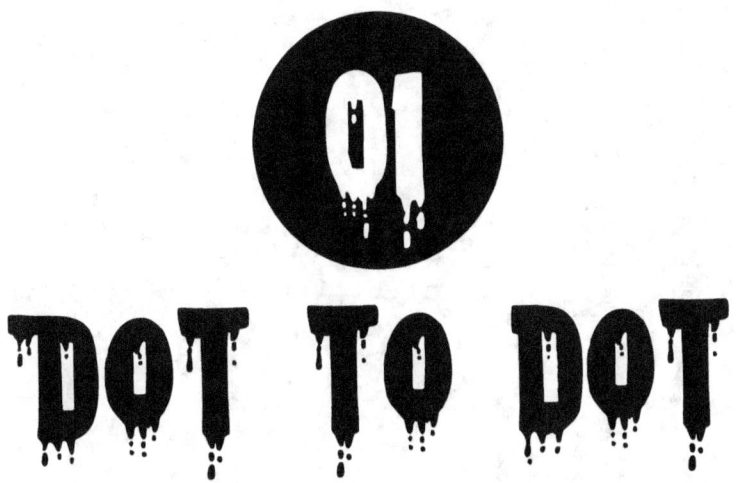

DOT TO DOT

Dot-to-dots, also called connect-the-dots or join-the-dots, are a fun, involving a sequence of numbered dots that are connected one by one by drawing a line, revealing a fun picture.

Try 2 methods:

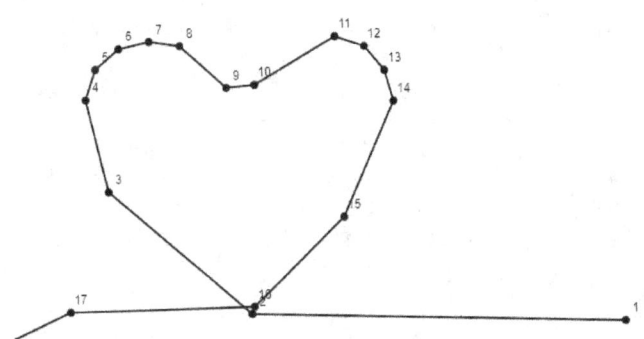

"Geometric" Style

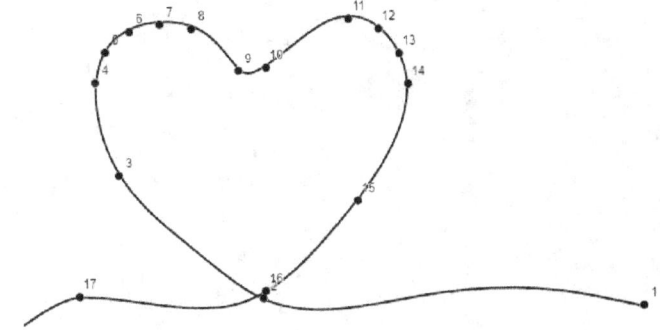

"Smooth" Style

Let's start!

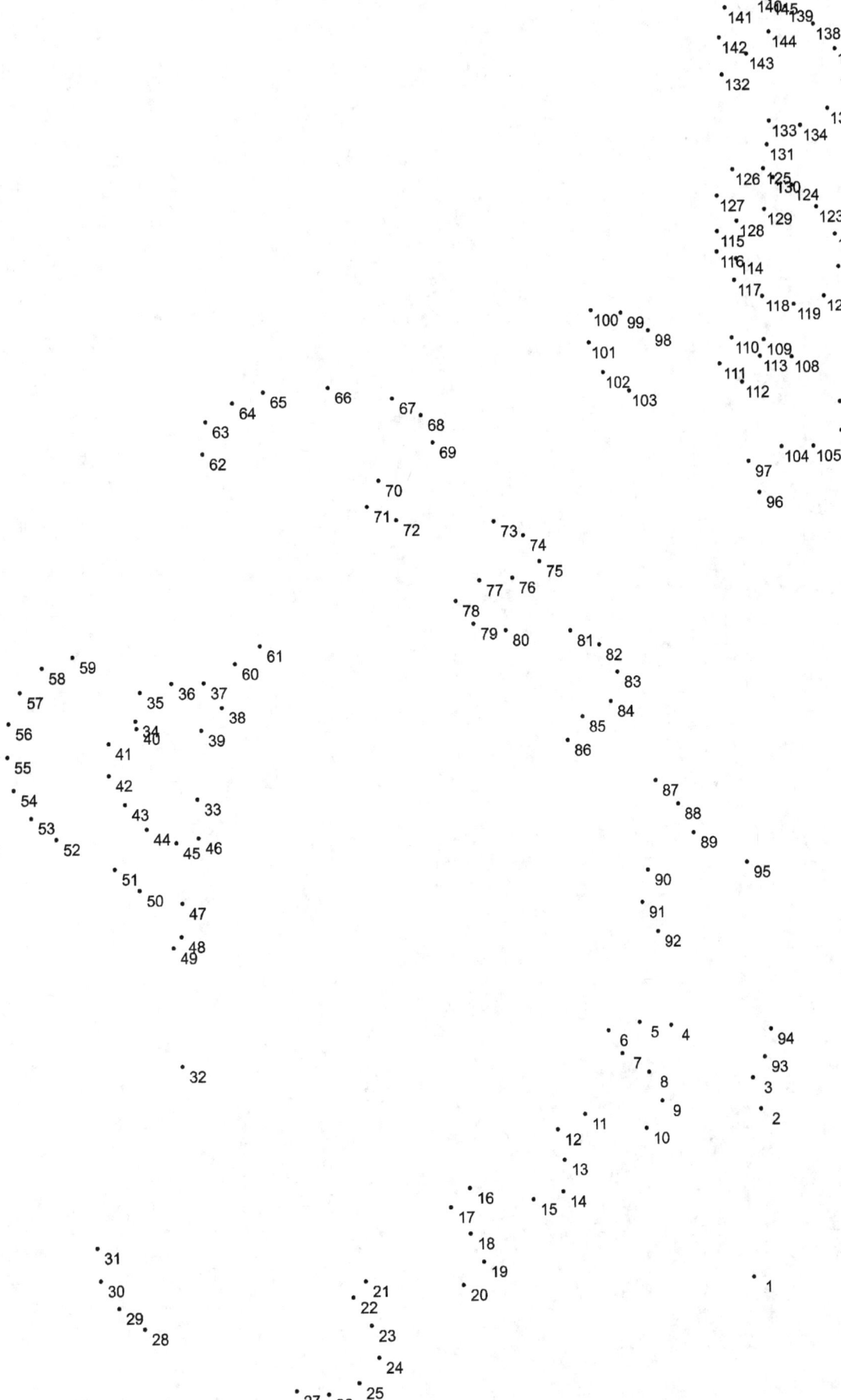

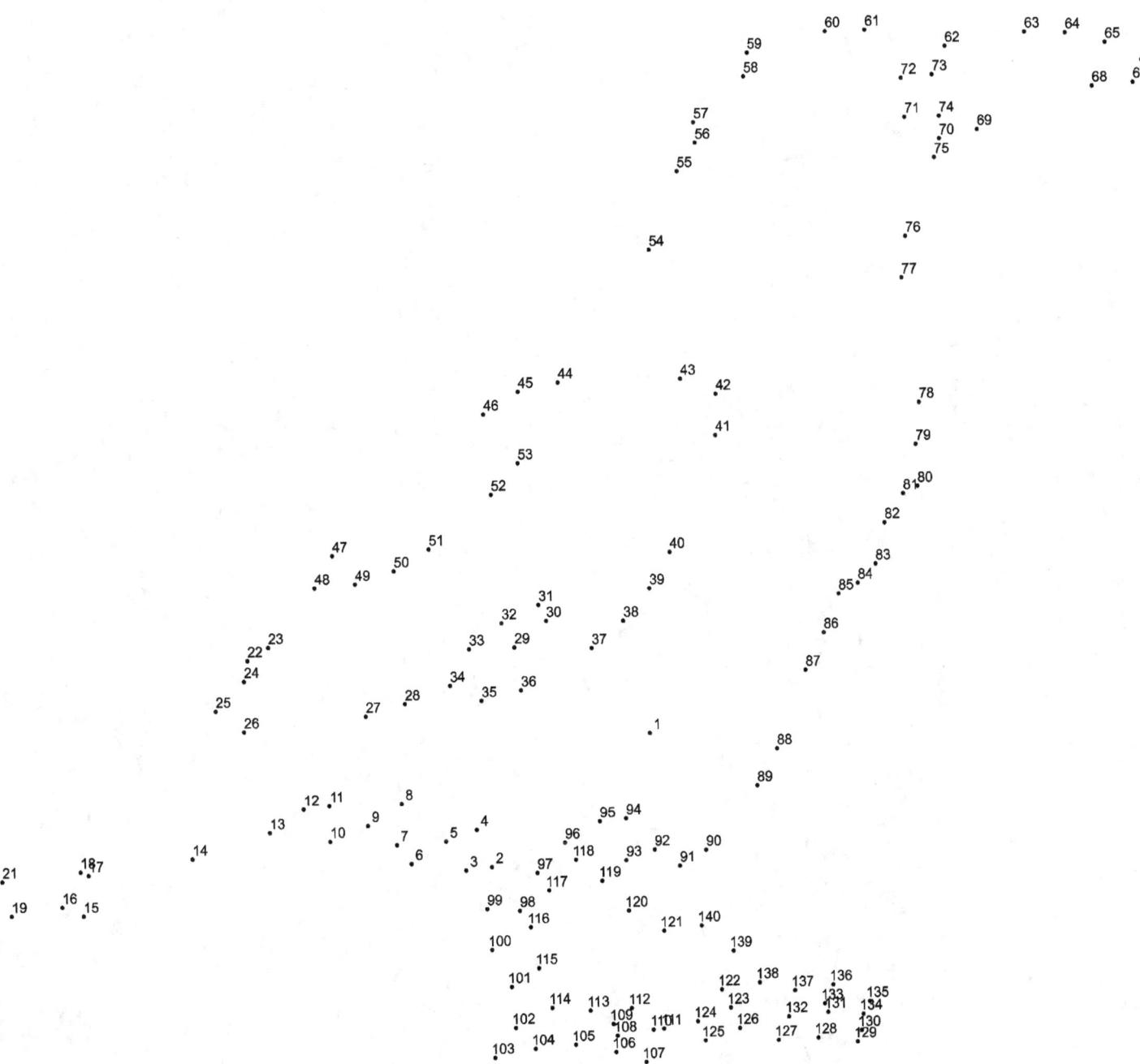

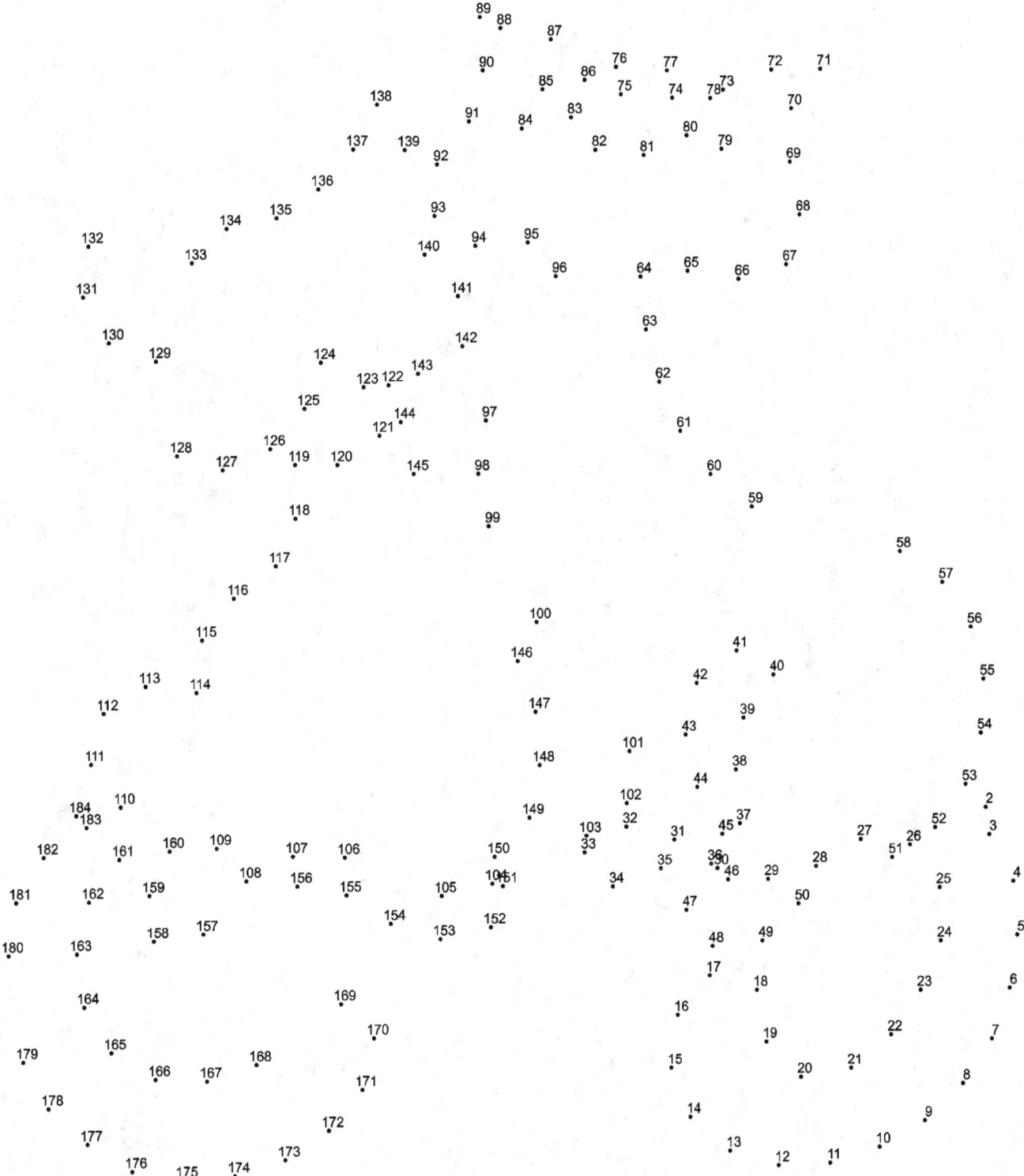

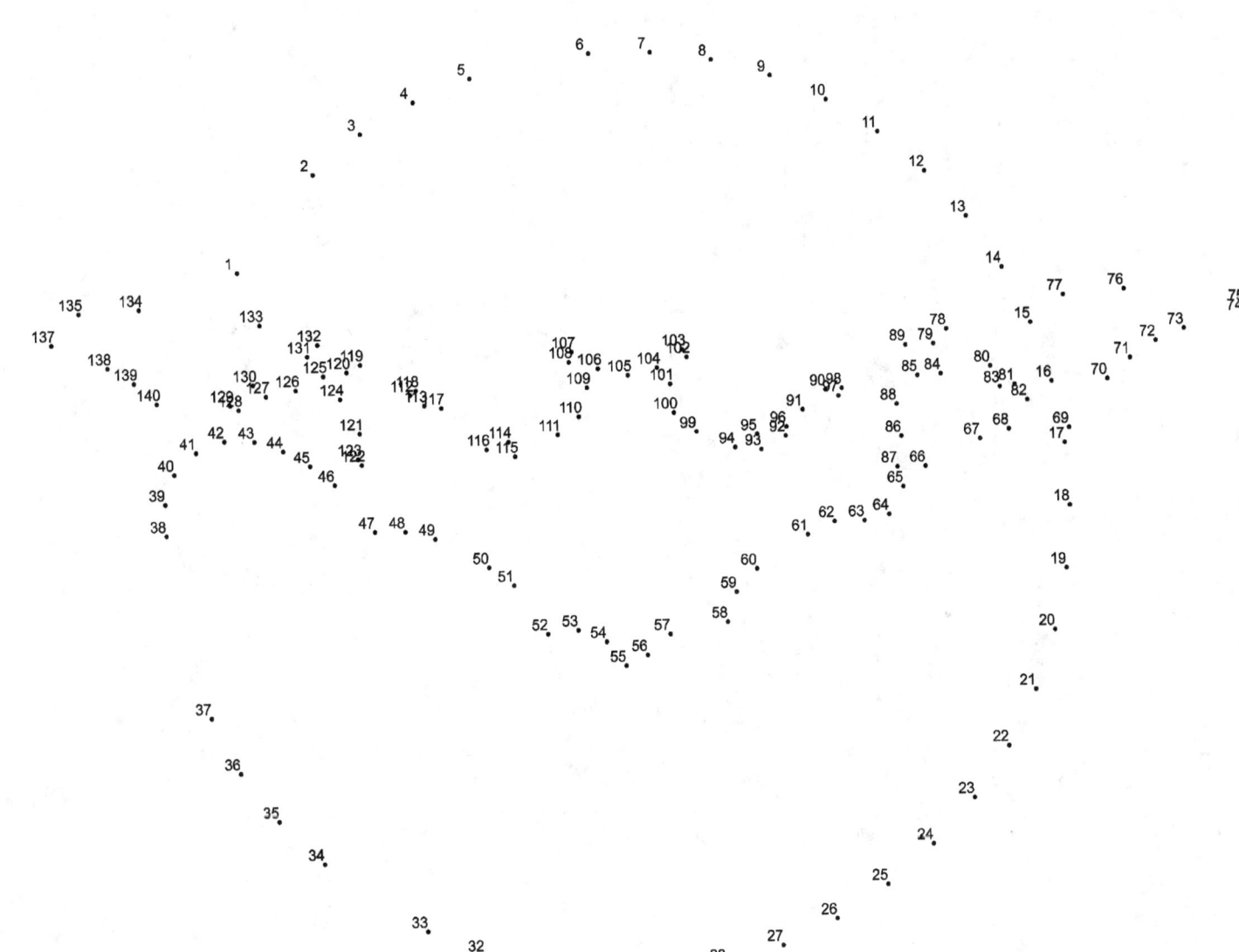

HINTS

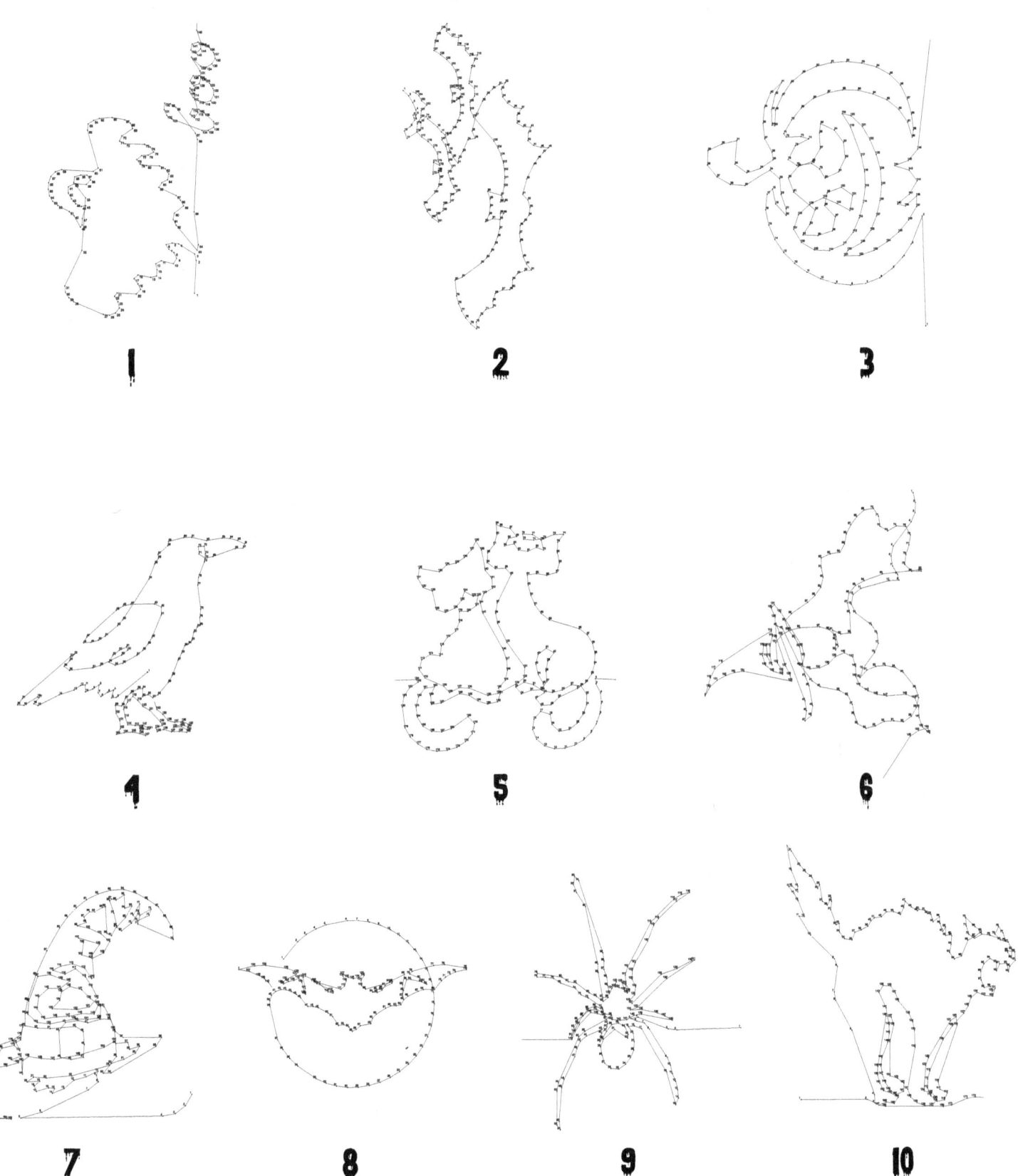

iF YOU WANT TO TRY A NEW METHOD

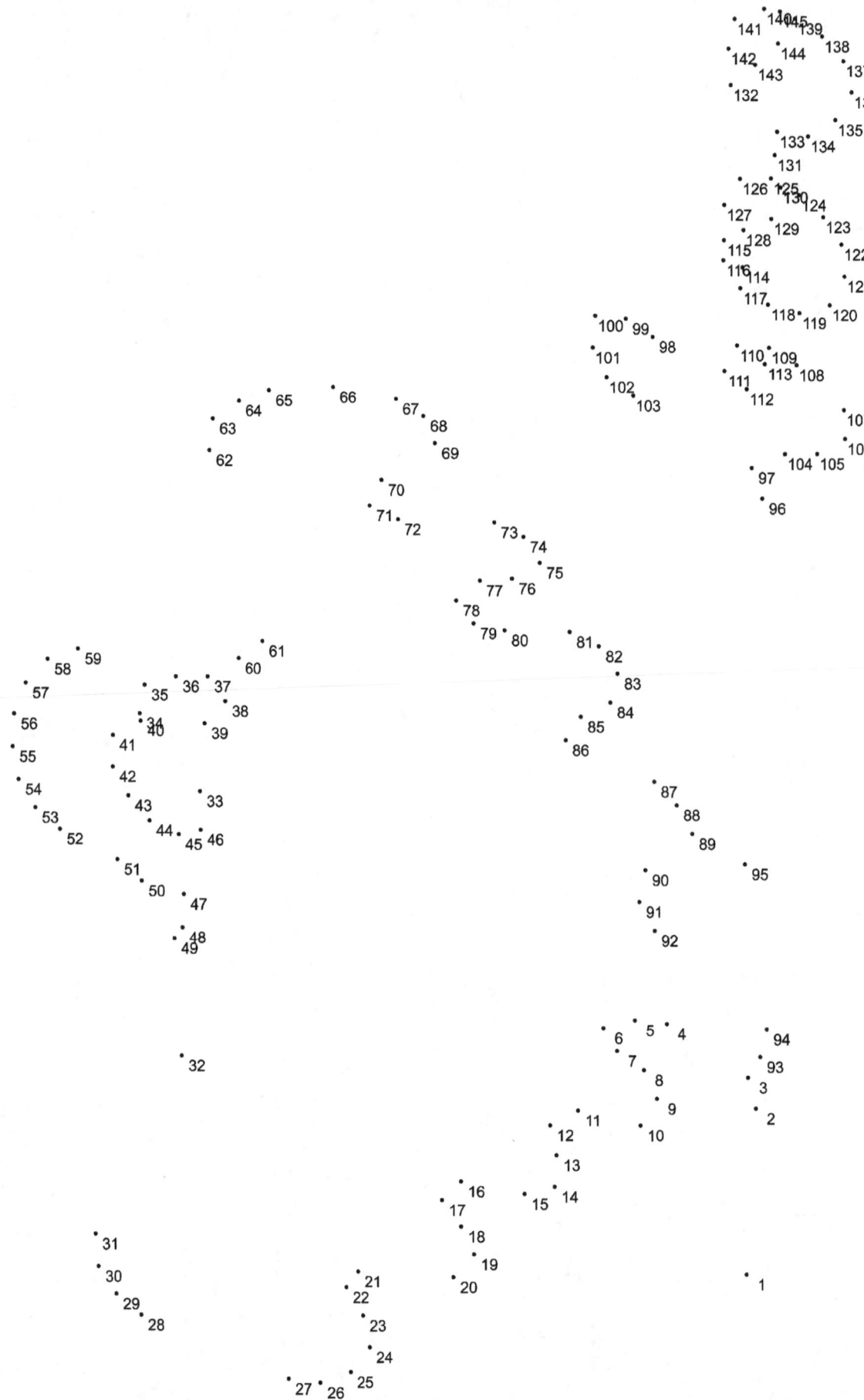

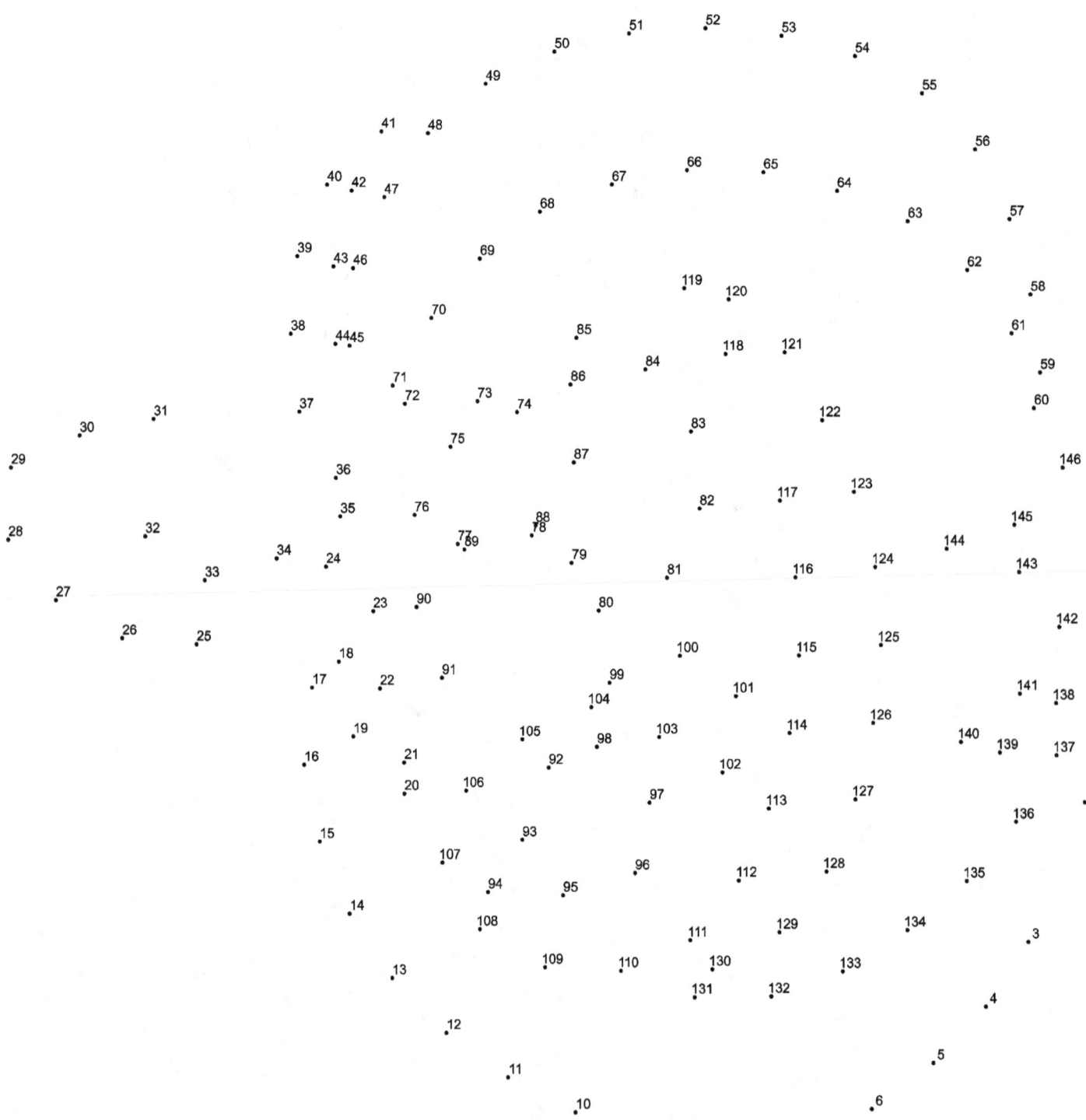

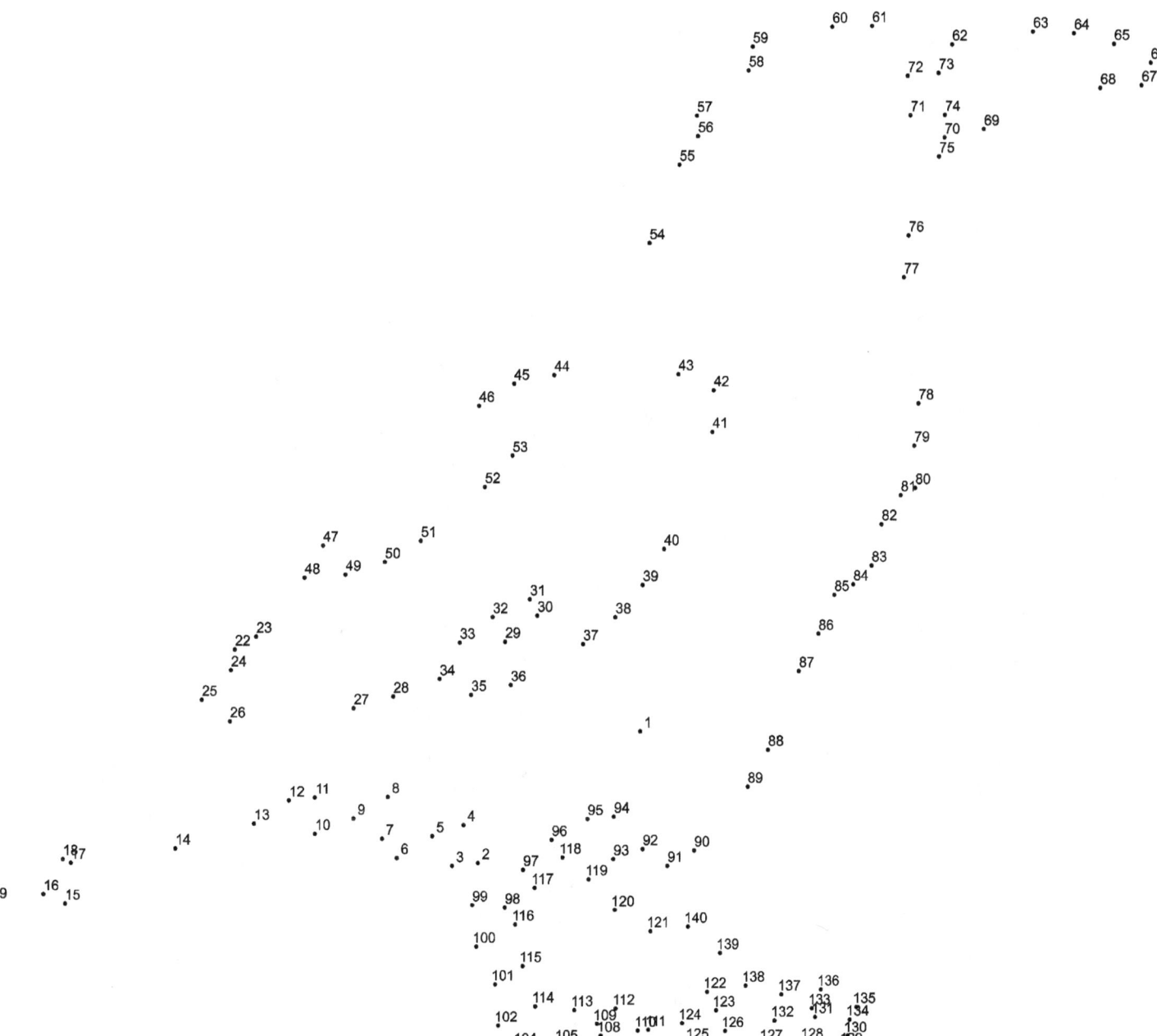

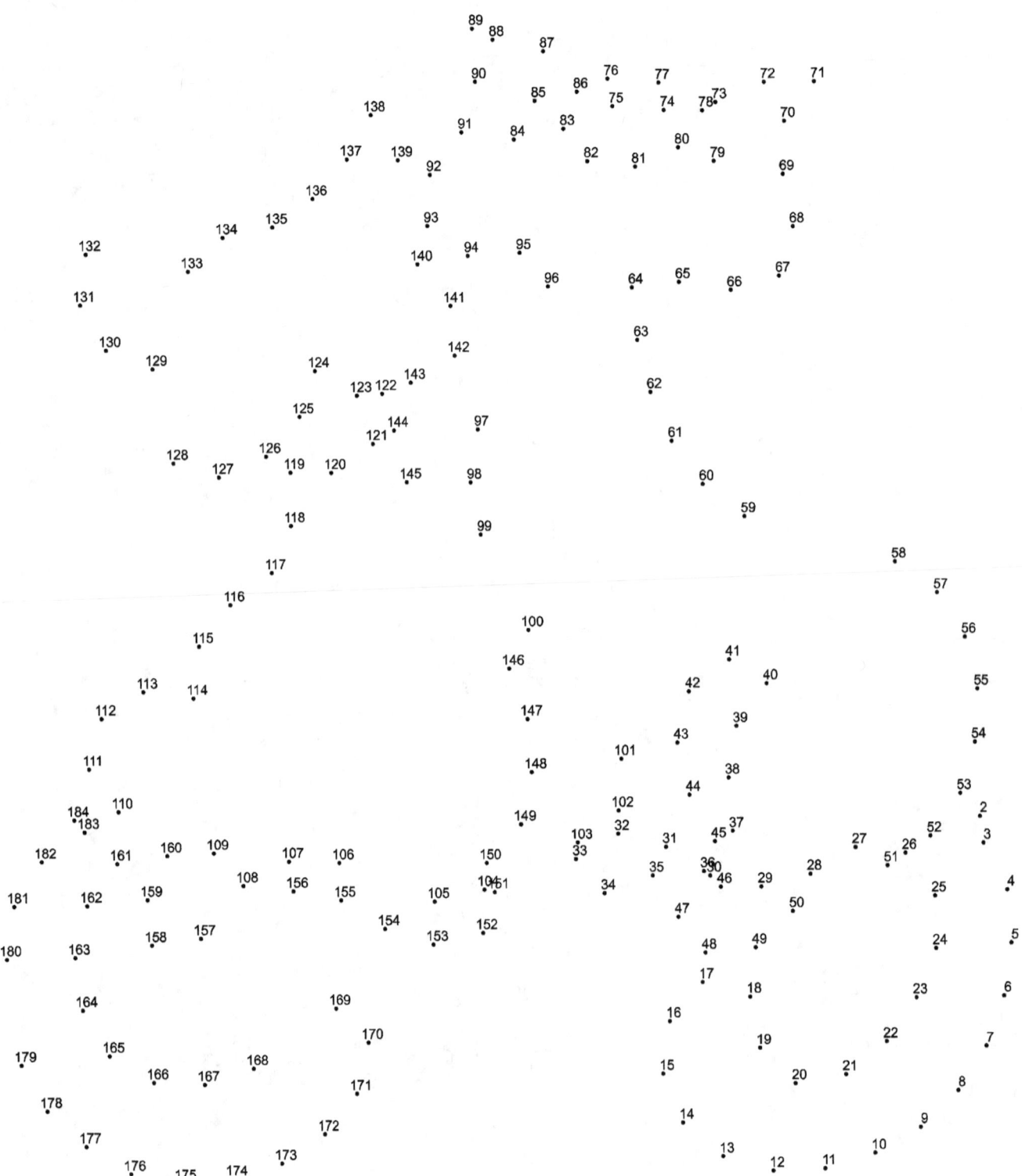

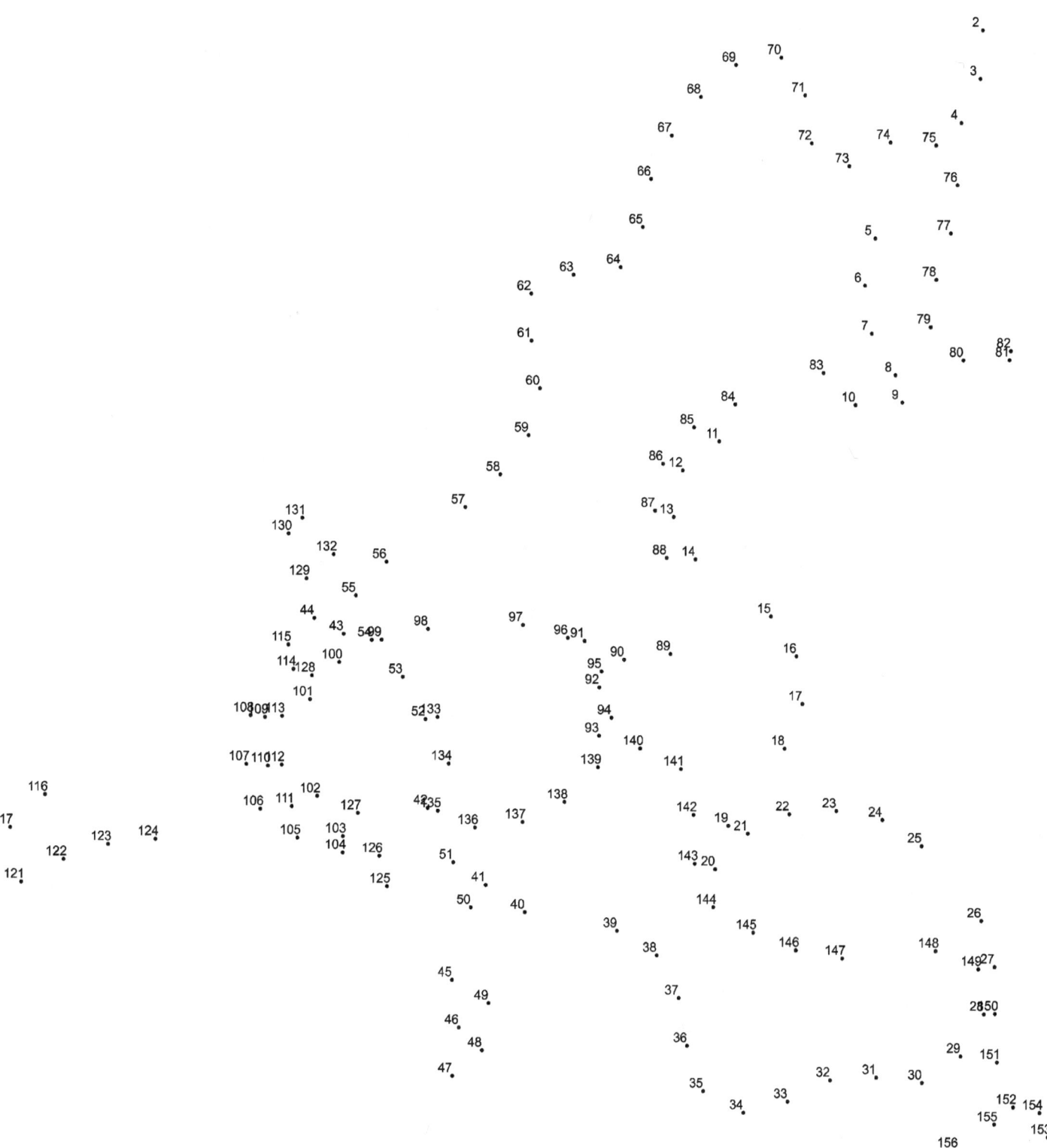

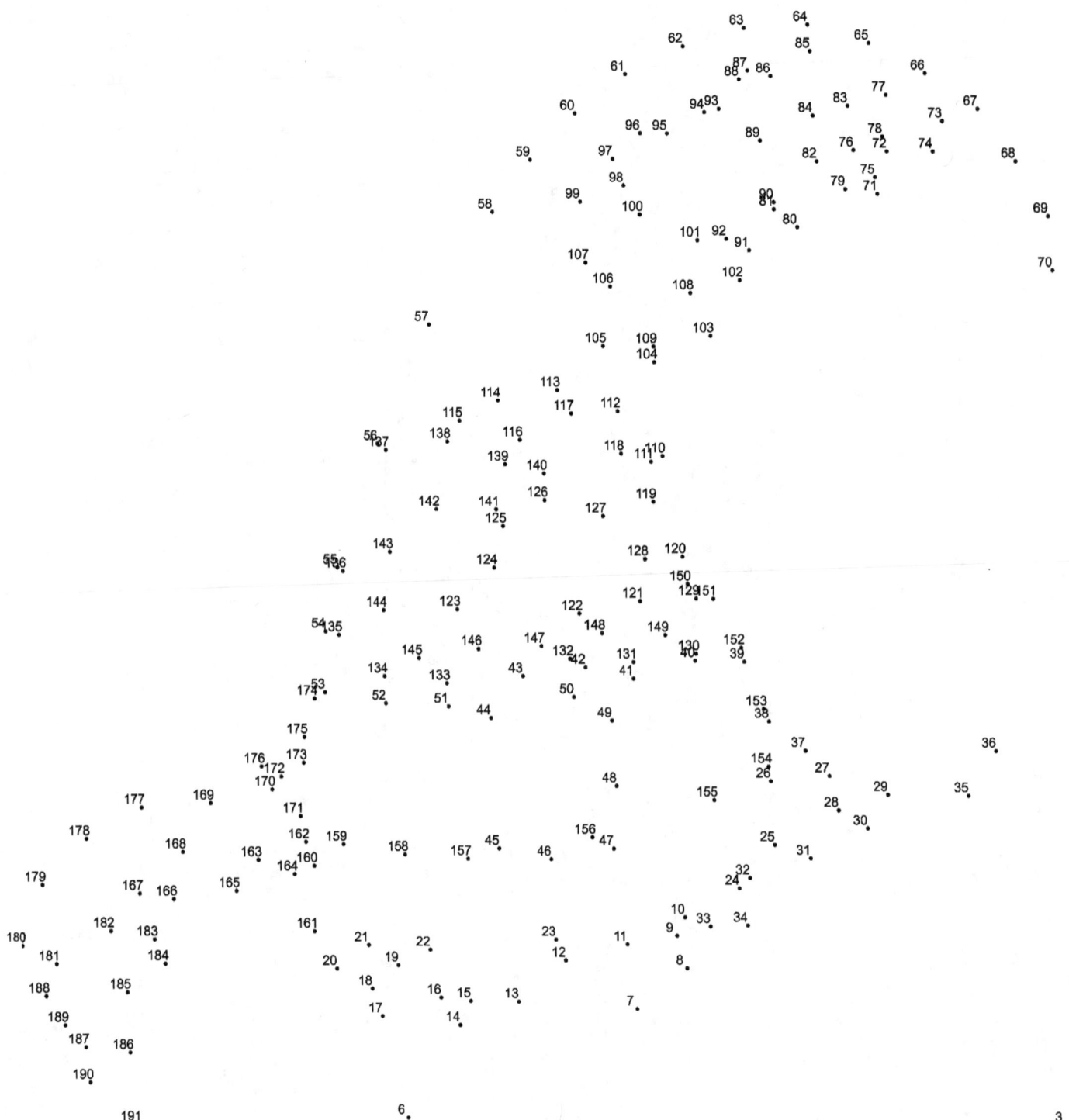

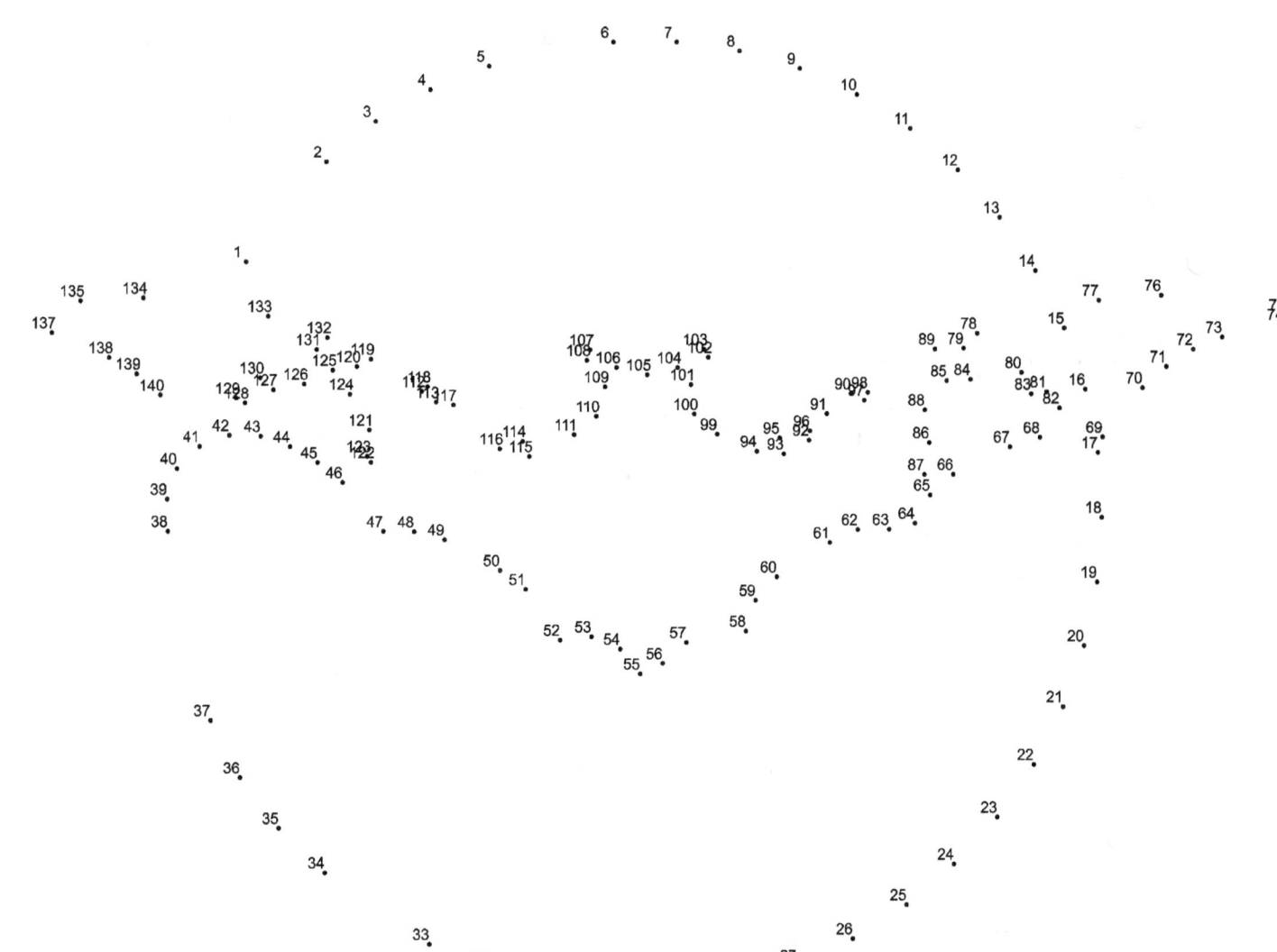

02
PIXEL COLOR

It's easy! Just choose colors in the palette and color cells with matching numbers pixel by pixel. Only 2 or 3 colors need to fill.

Try 2 methods:

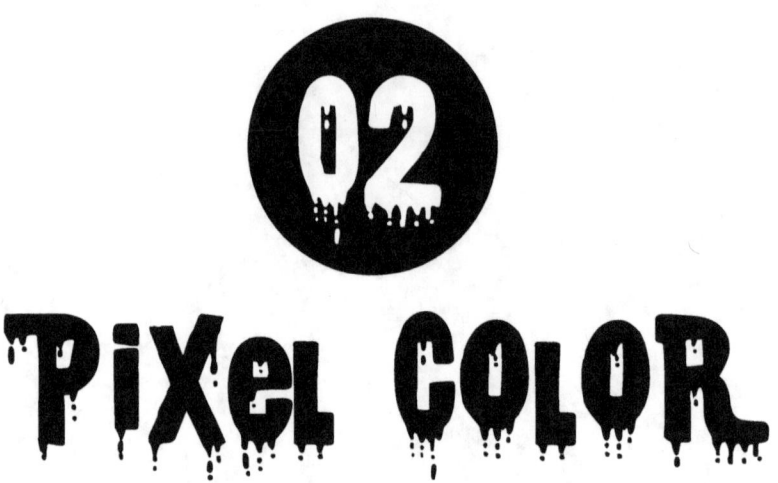

Color Pallette:
2 = BLACK
0 = WHITE

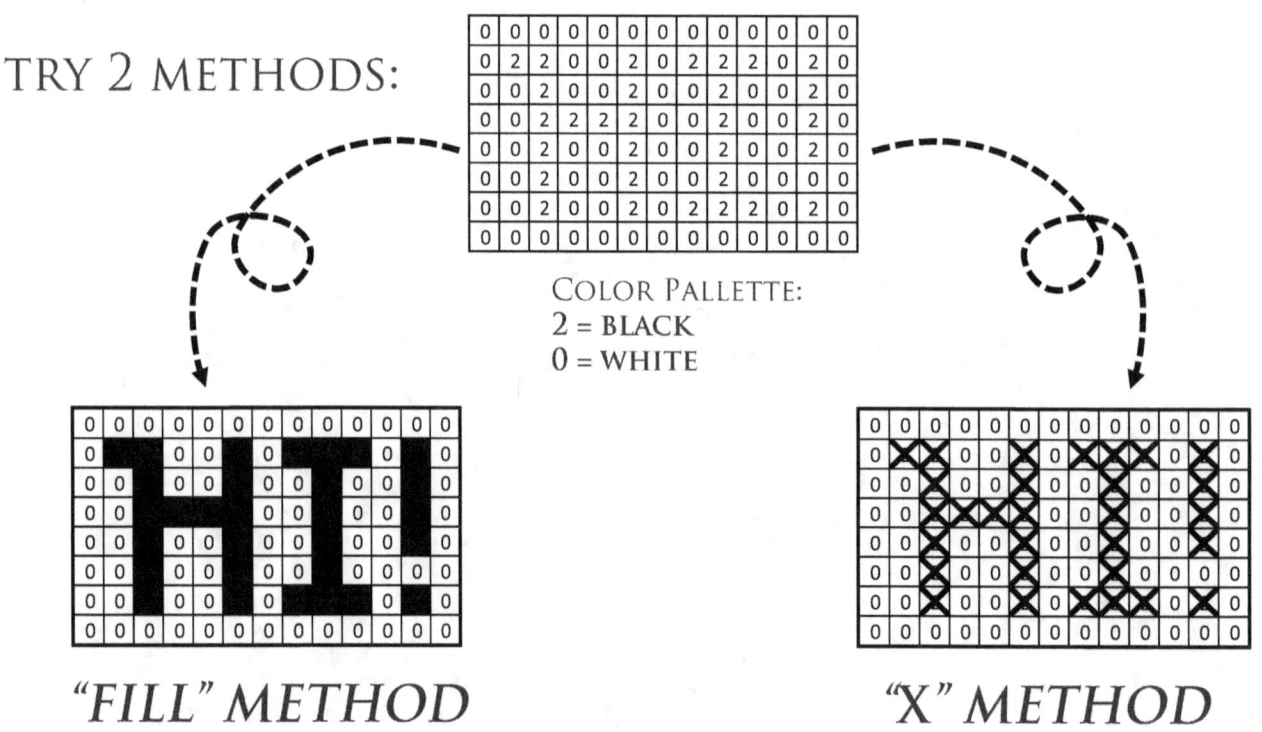

"FILL" METHOD   "X" METHOD

LET'S START!

COLOR PALLETTE:
1 = BLACK   0 = WHITE

9 = BLACK   0 = WHITE

1 = BLACK   7 = WHITE

8 = BLACK   0 = WHITE

9 = BLACK   6 = WHITE

8 = BLACK   3 = WHITE

1 = BLACK   2 = ORANGE   0 = WHITE

1 = BLACK   2 = ORANGE   0 = WHITE

5 = BLACK   2 = ORANGE   6 = WHITE

7 = BLACK   4 = ORANGE   1 = WHITE

HINTS

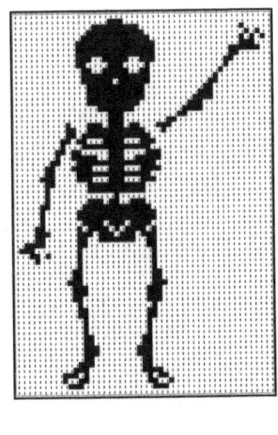

1

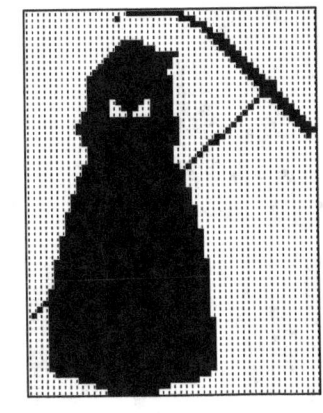

2

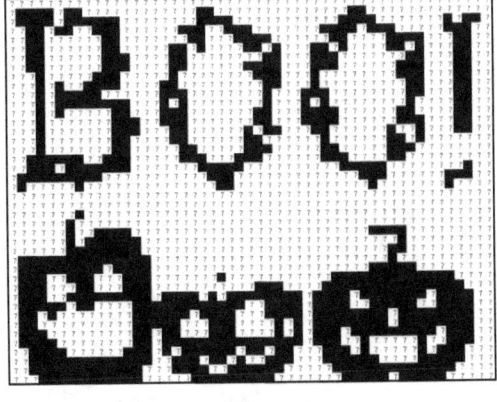

3

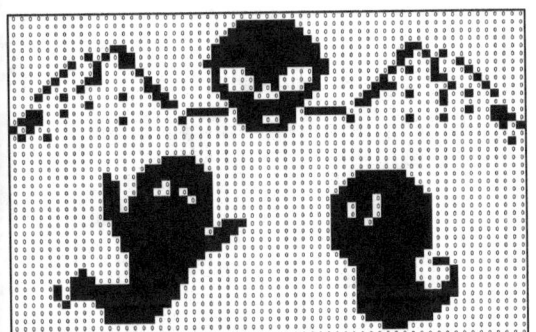

4

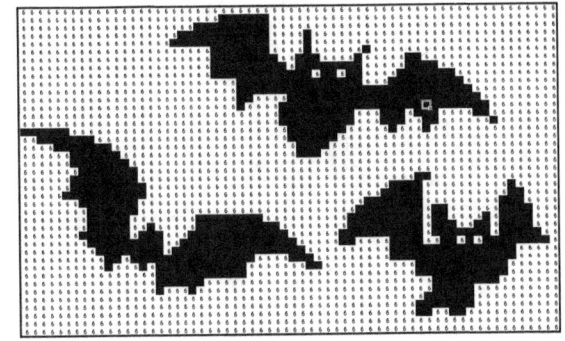

5

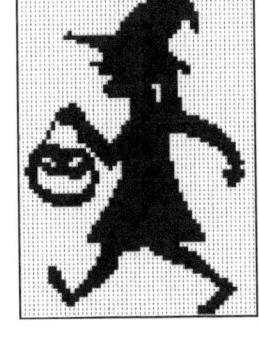

6

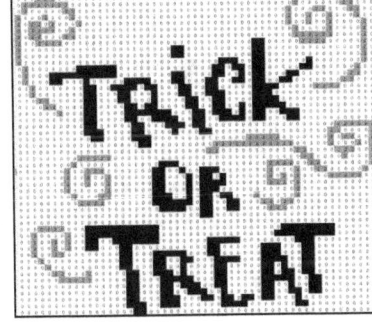

7

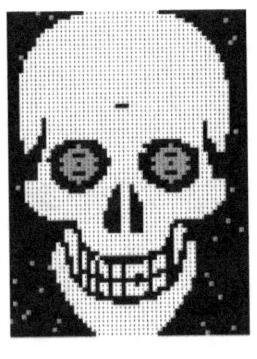

8

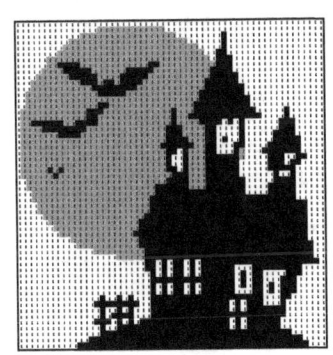

9

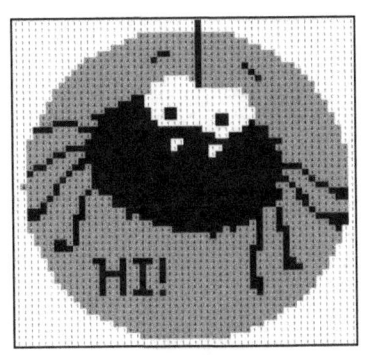

10

03
COLORING PAGES

Enjoy your time ^^!

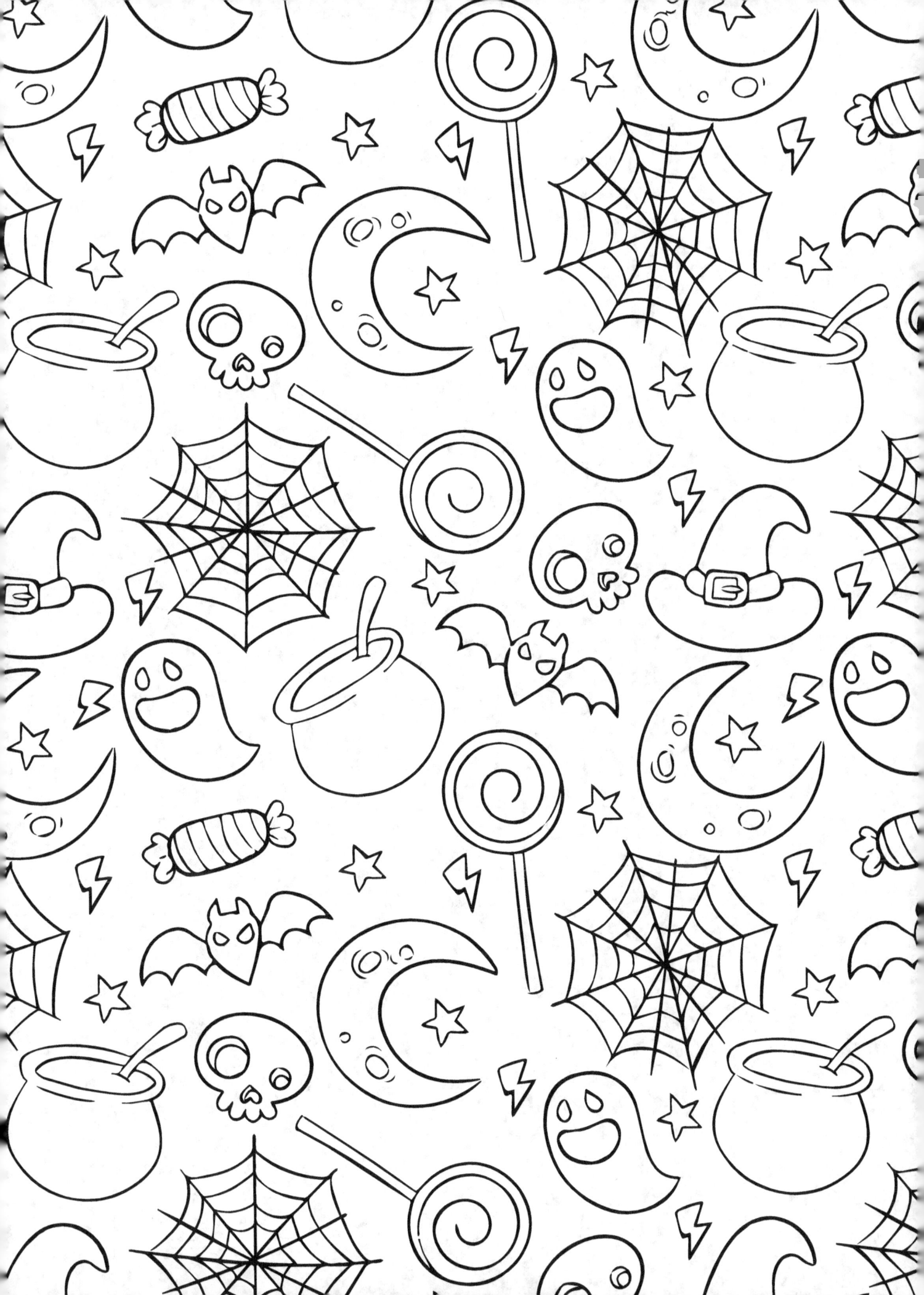

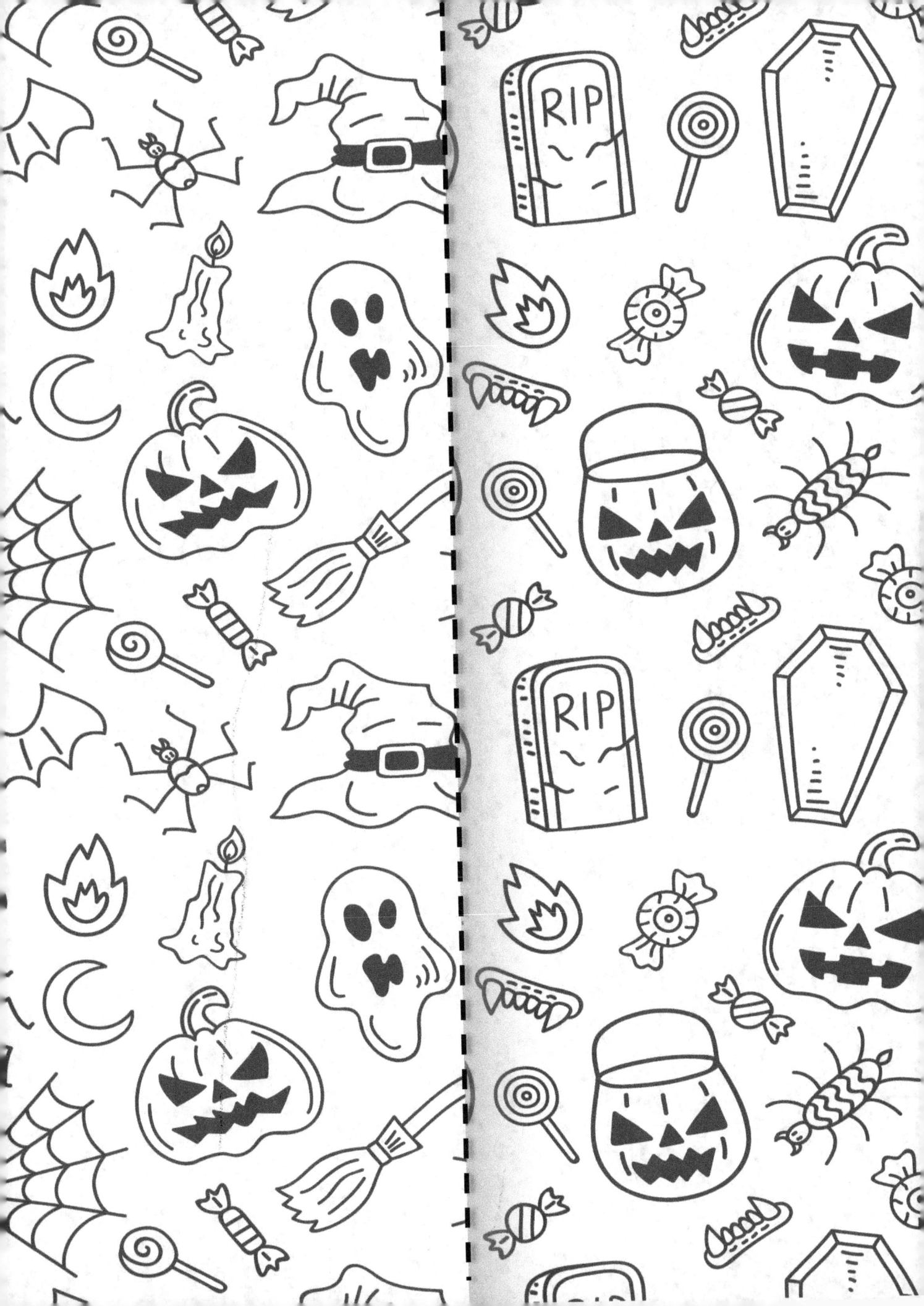

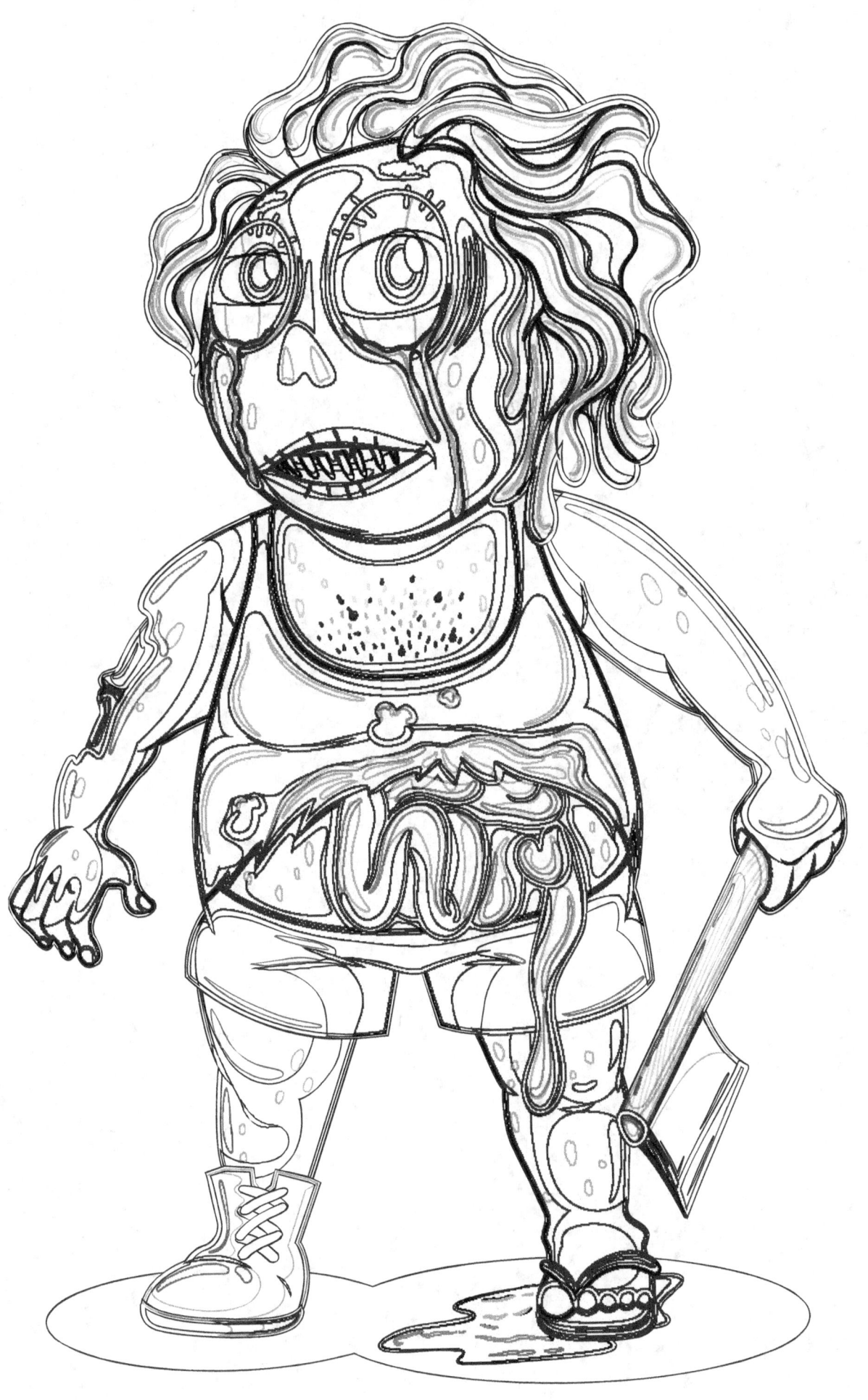

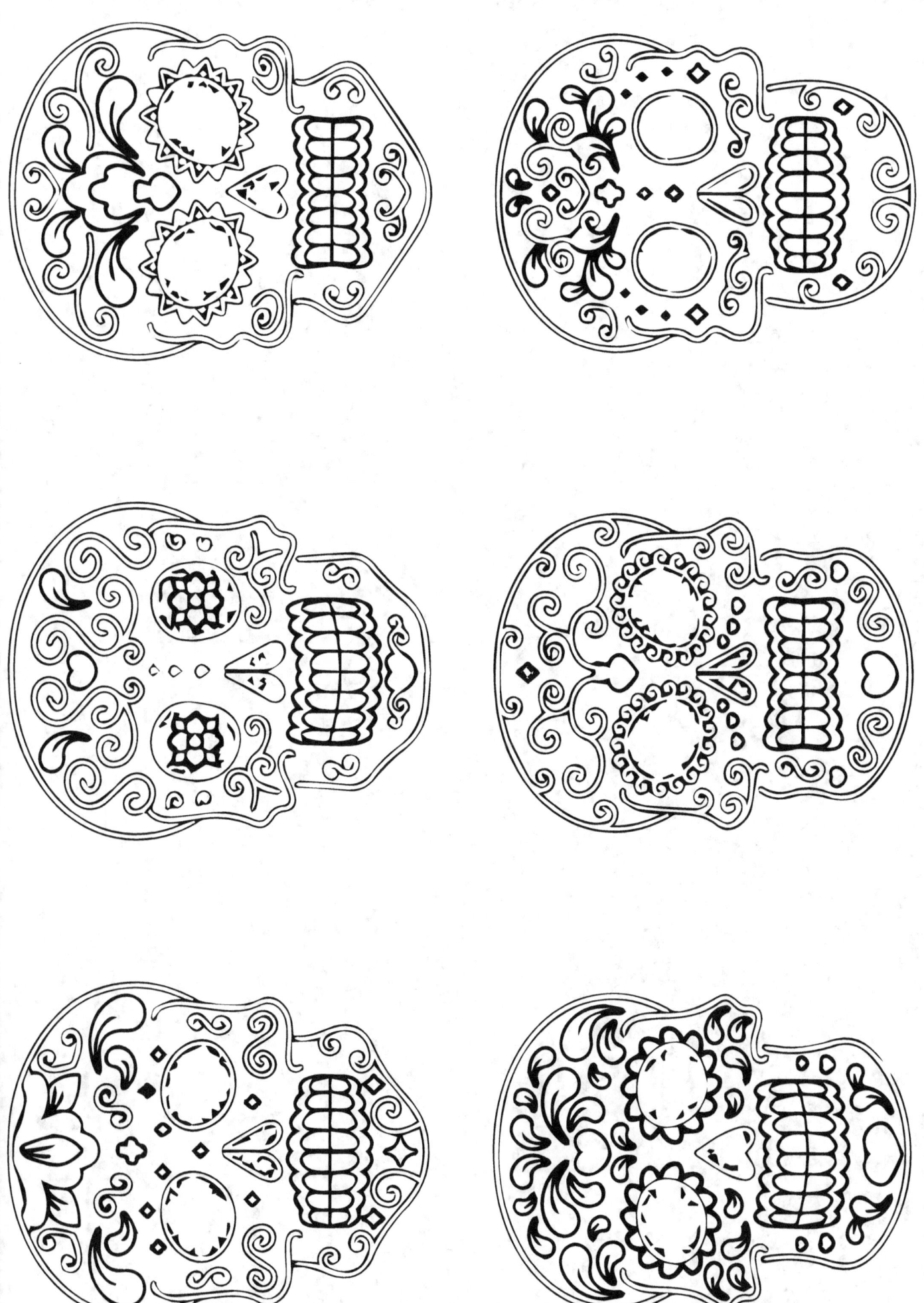

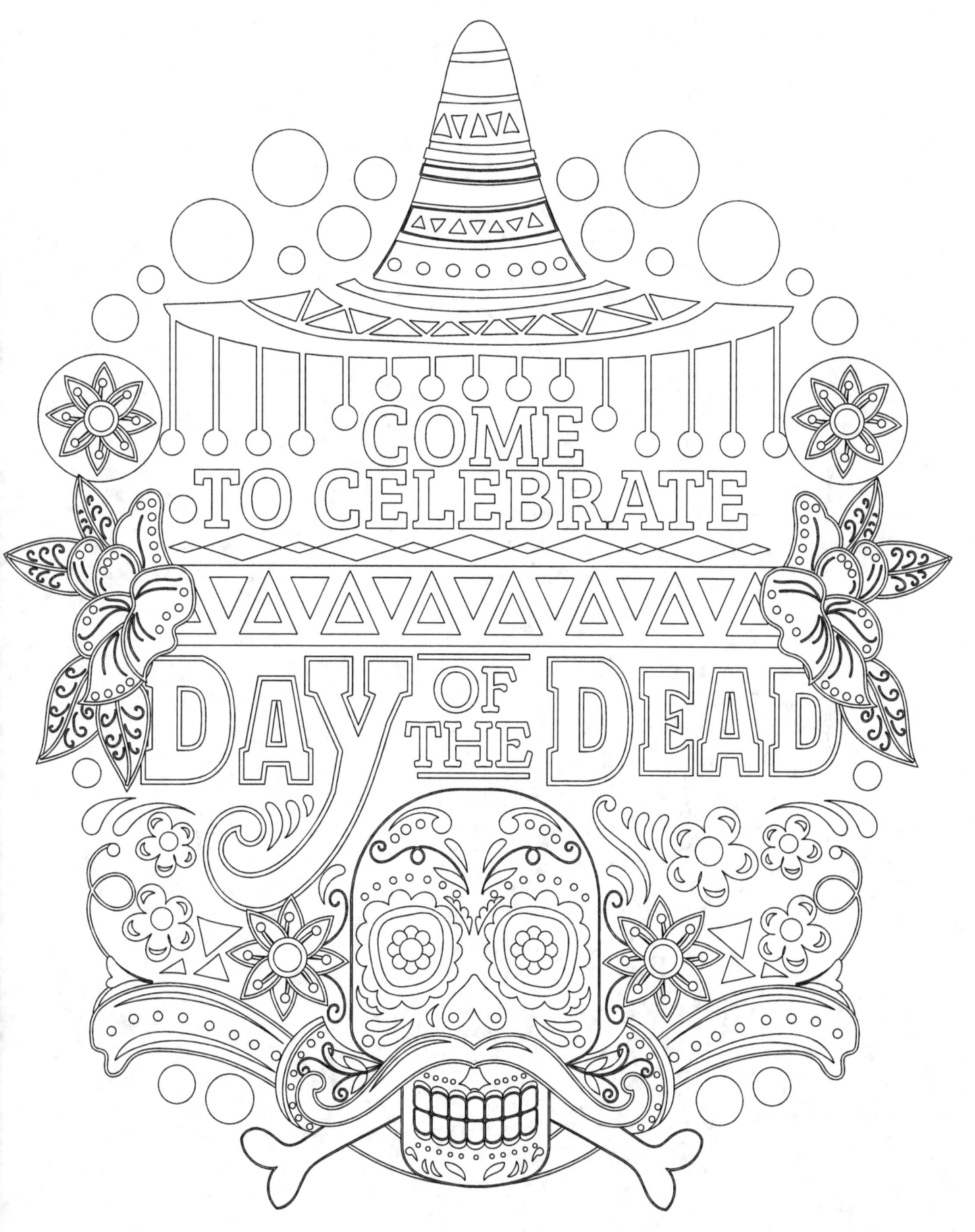

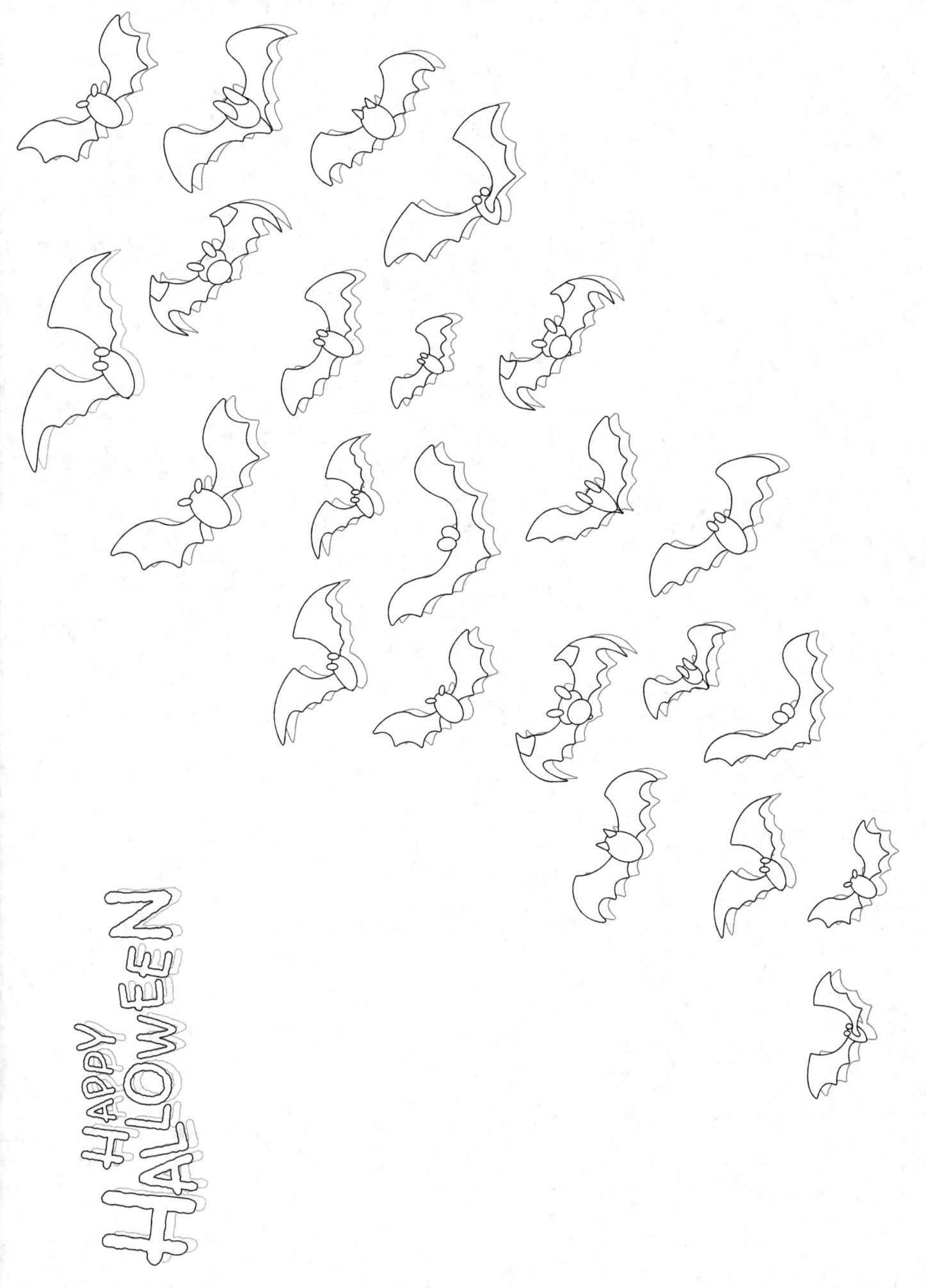

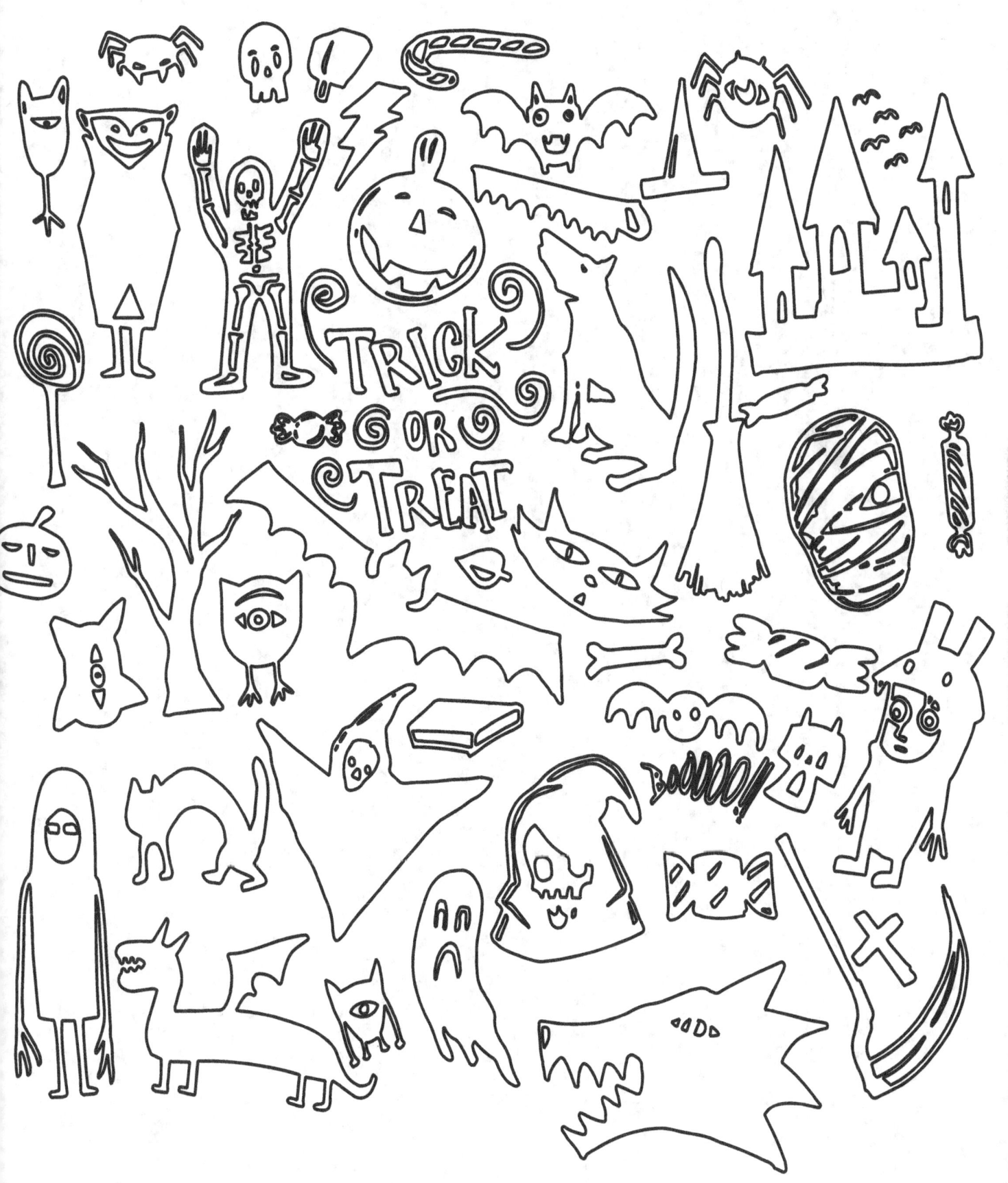

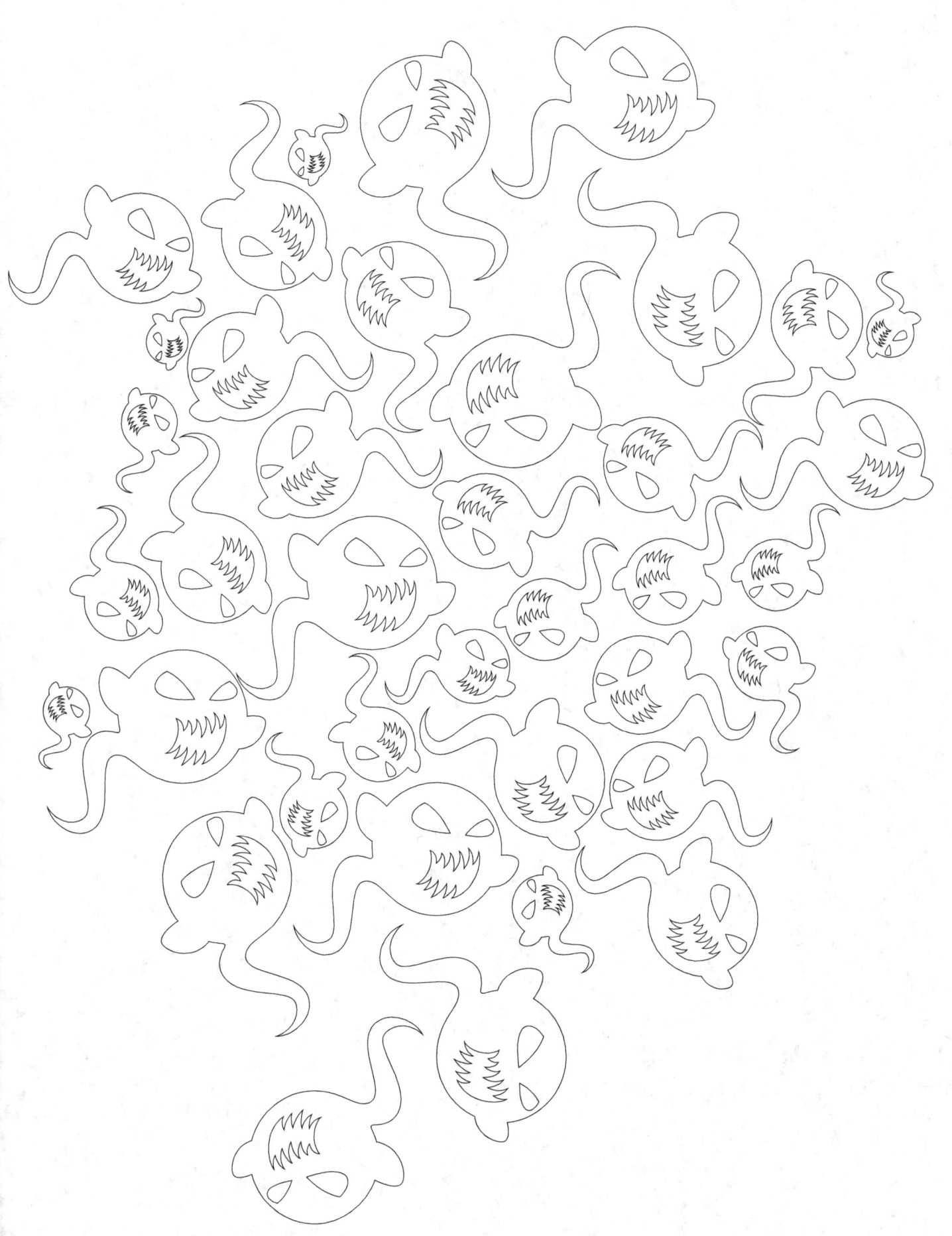

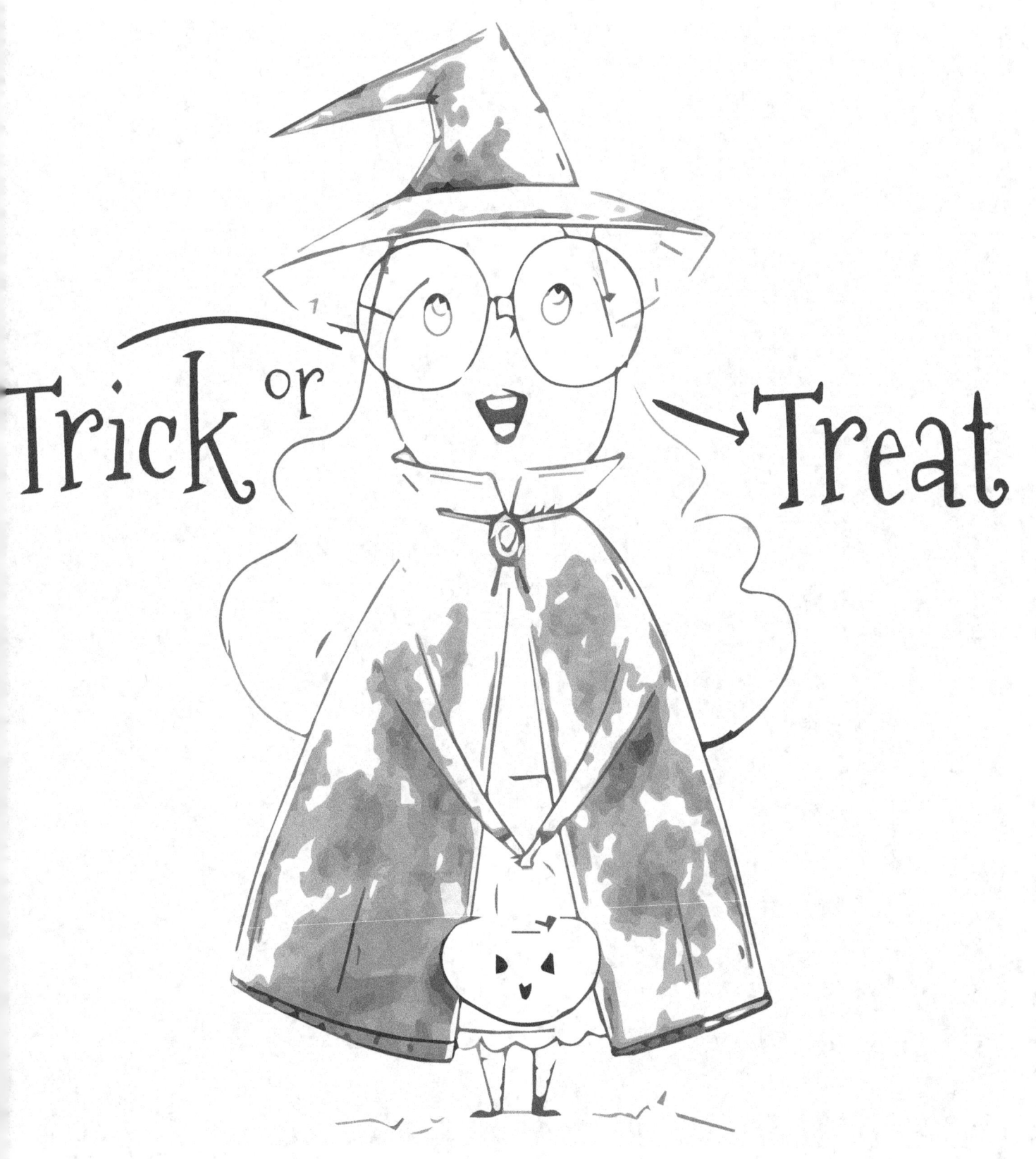

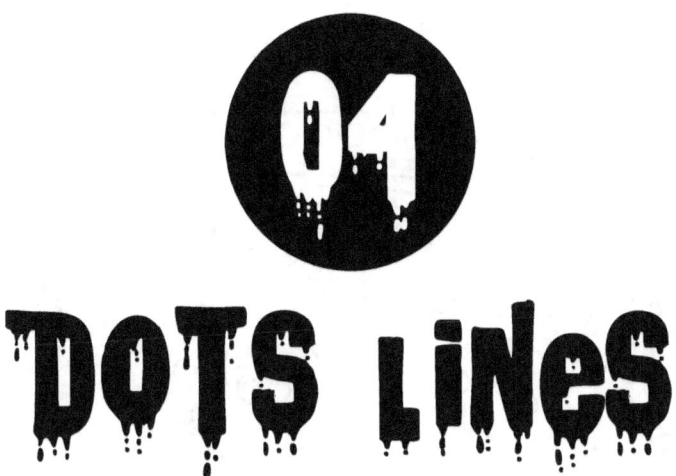

04
DOTS LINES

THAT'S EASY.
CHOOSE 1 COLOR, OR 2, 3 COLORS
FILL THE DOTS AND LINES WITH YOUR COLOR,
AND DISCOVERING "THE SECRET"

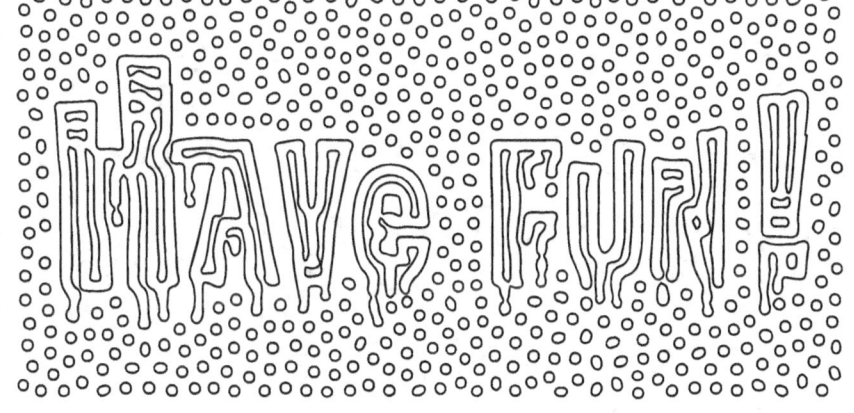

AFTER FILL

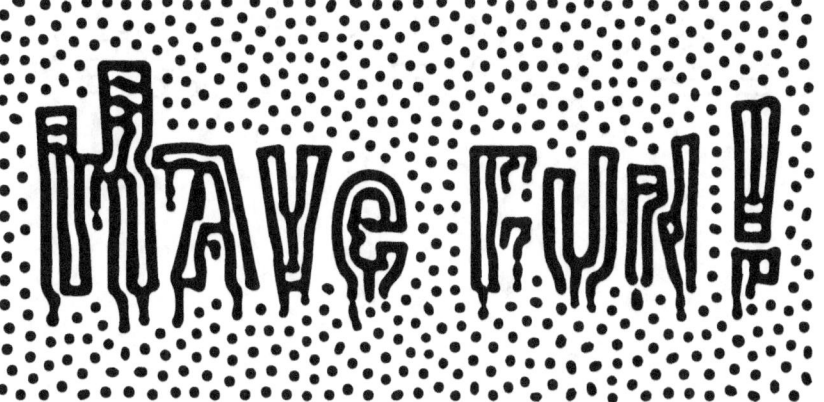

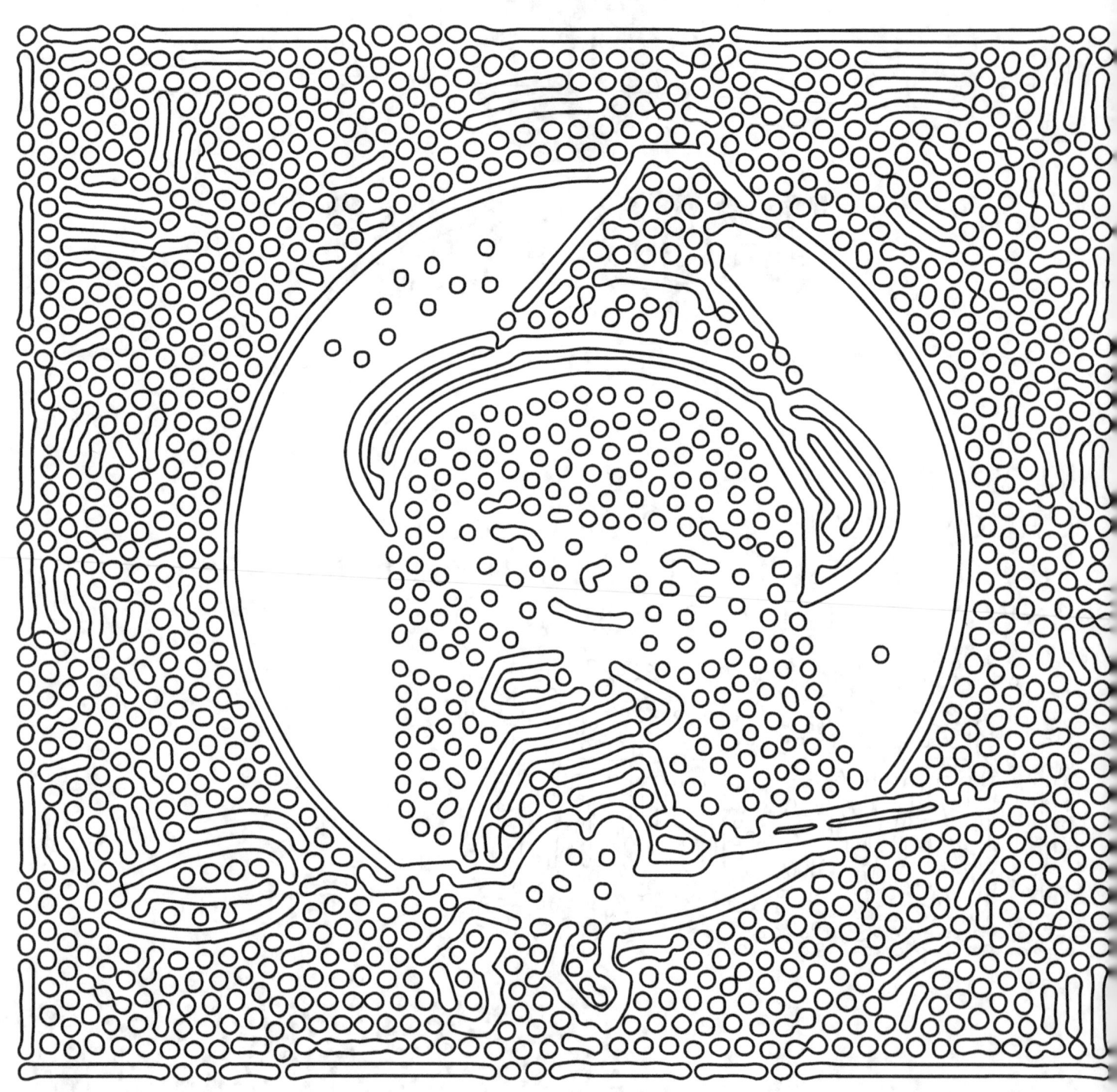

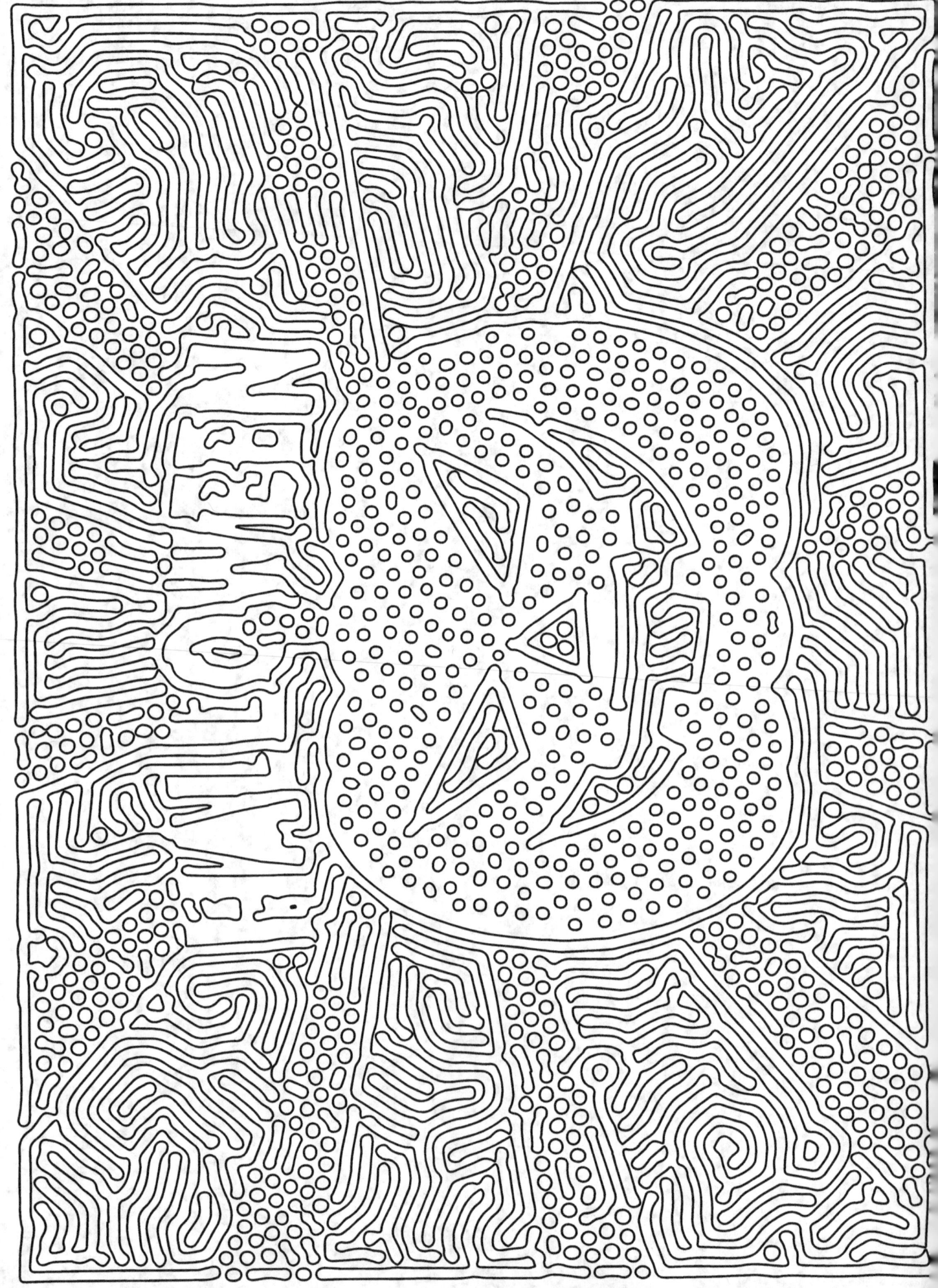

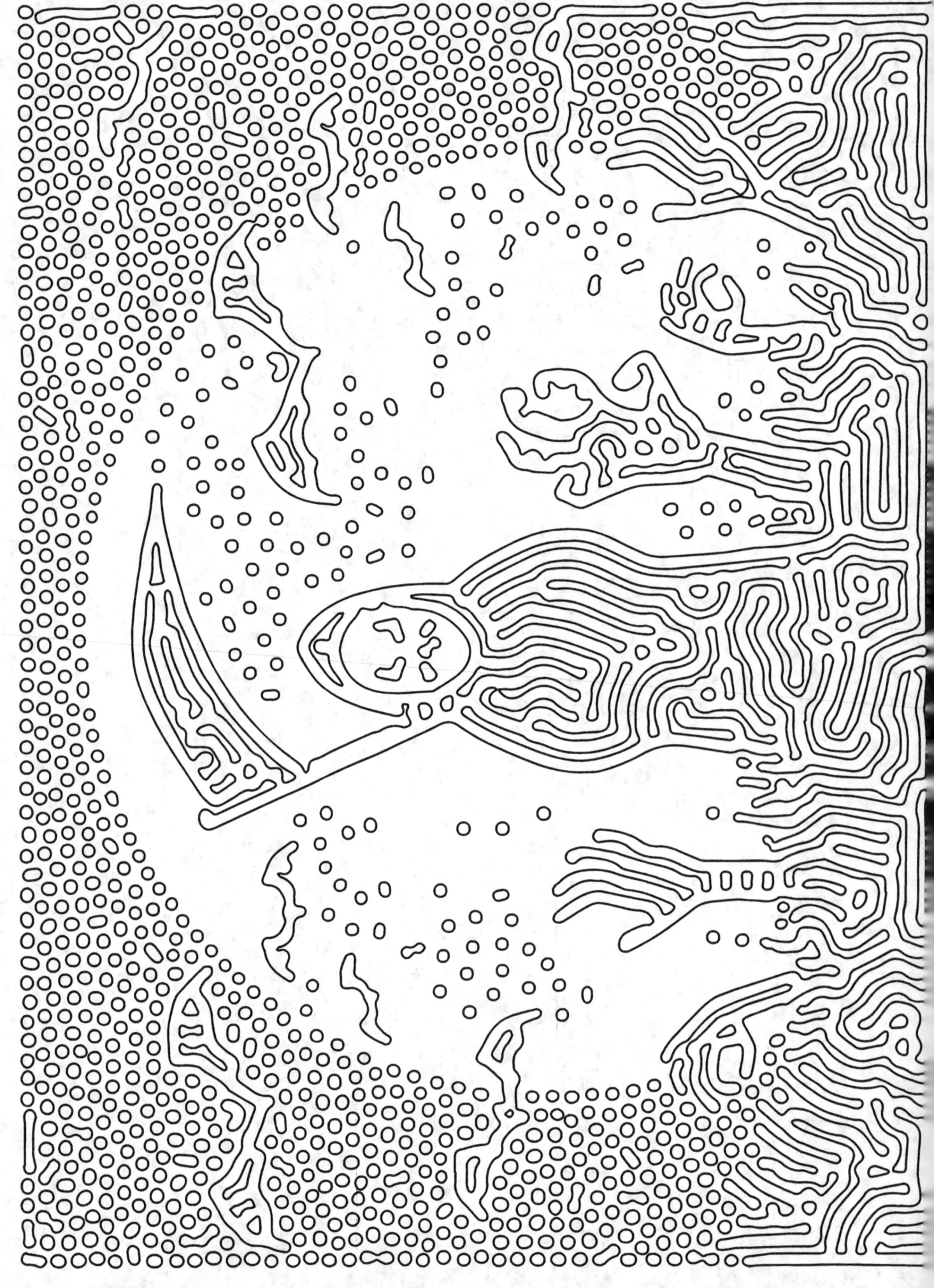

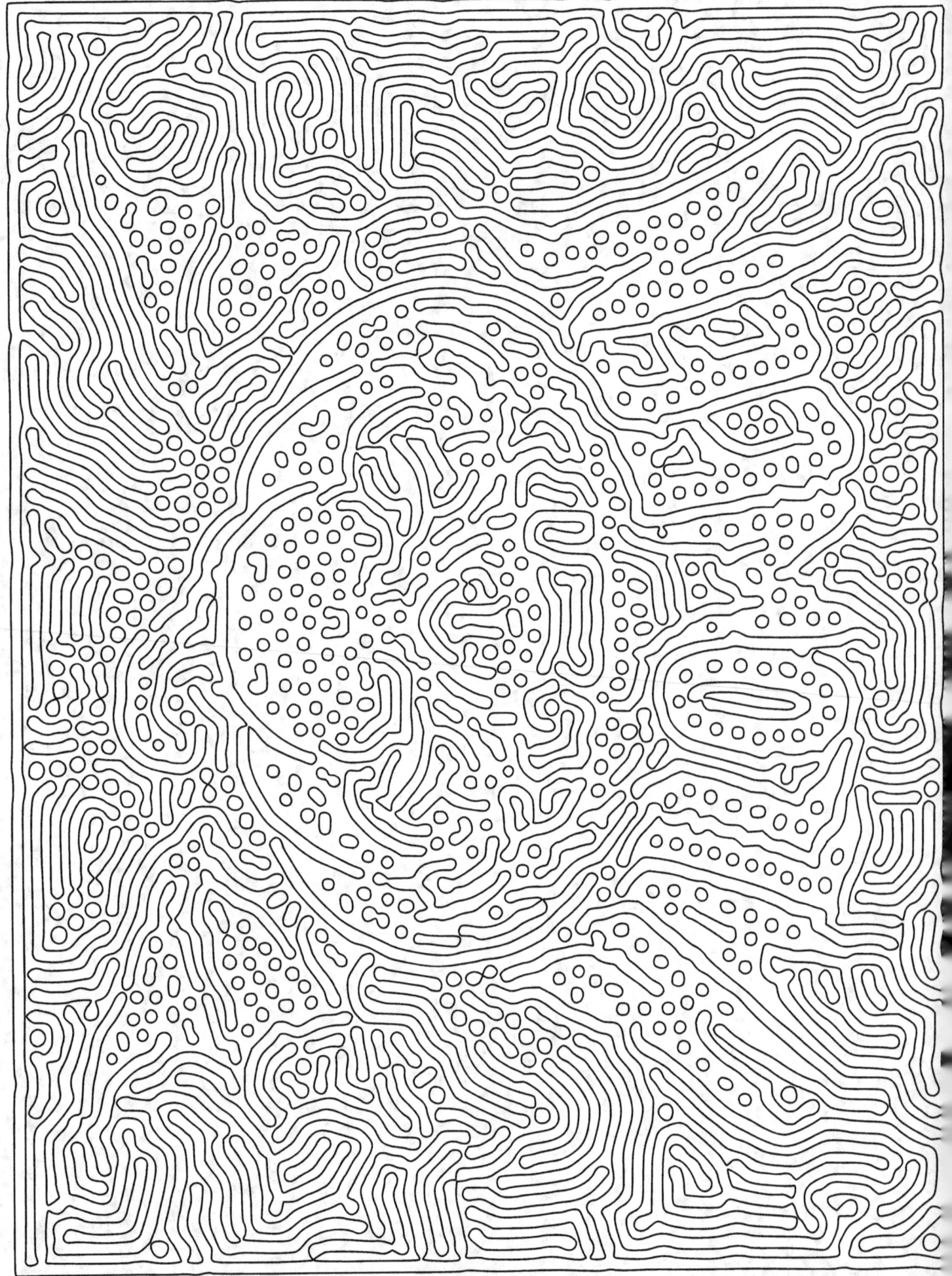

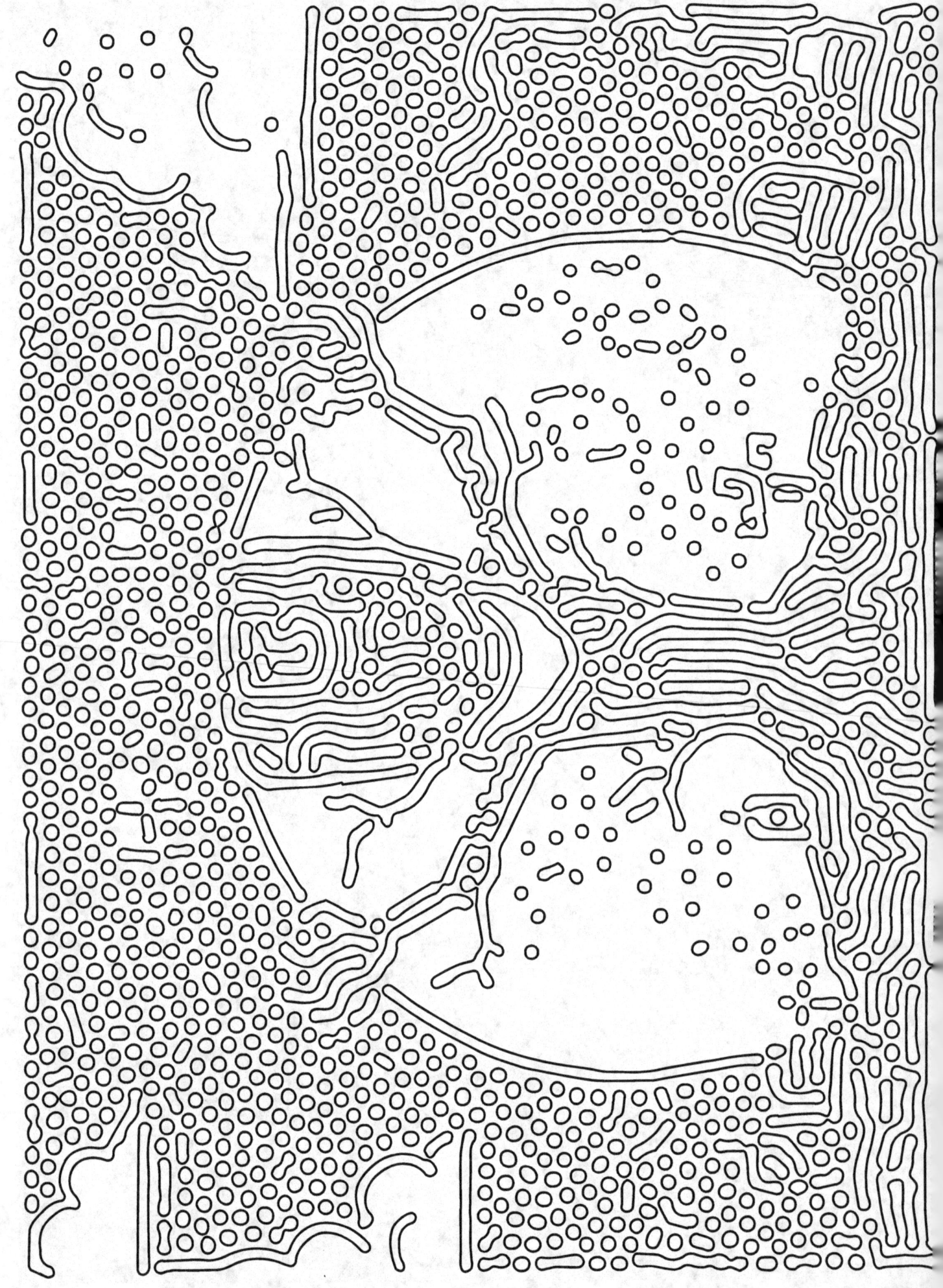

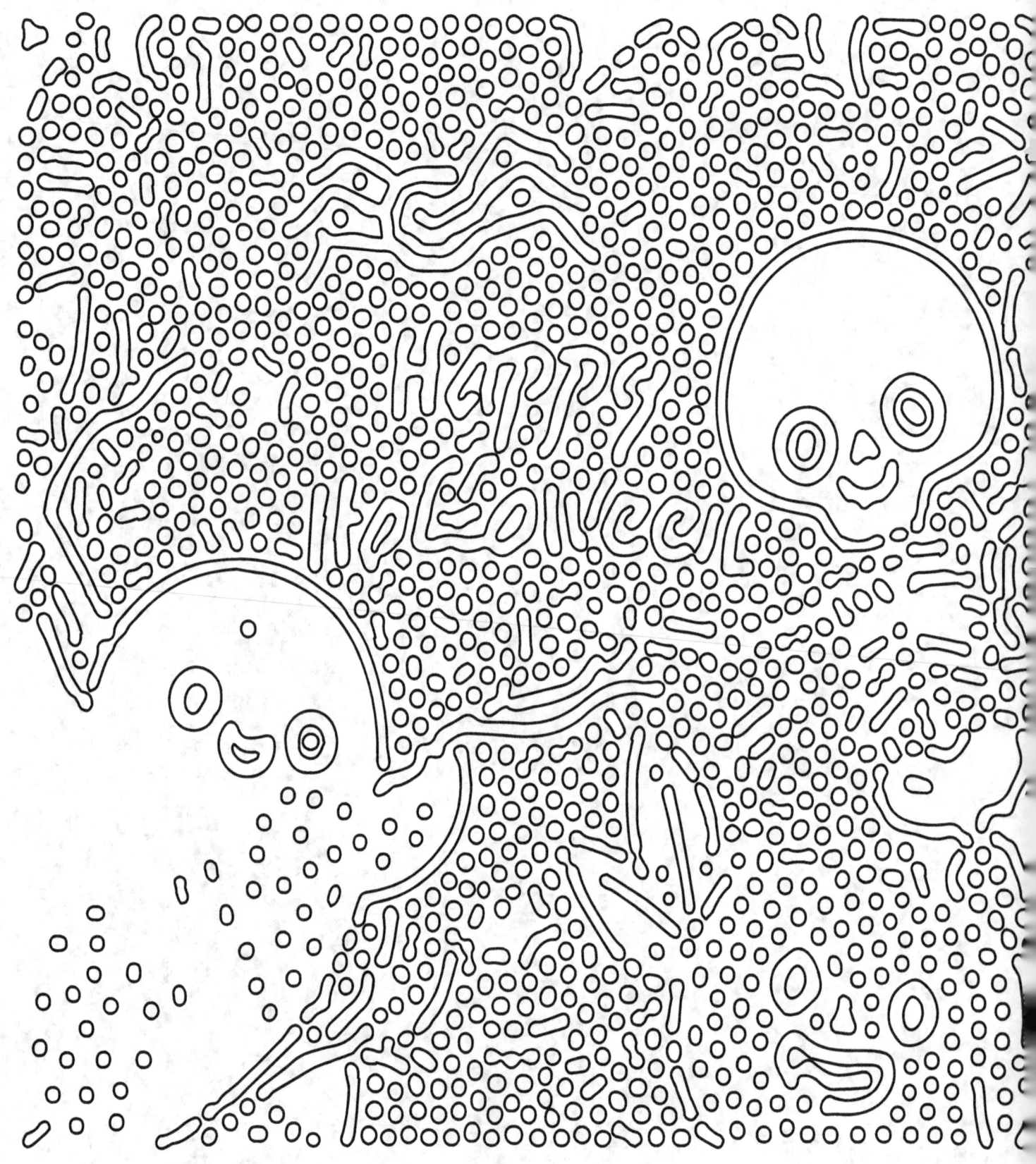

HINTS

THANK YOU,
AND
HAVE THRILLING FUN ON HALLOWEEN!

– OTHER BOOKS –

ONE COLOR DOTS LINES SERIES

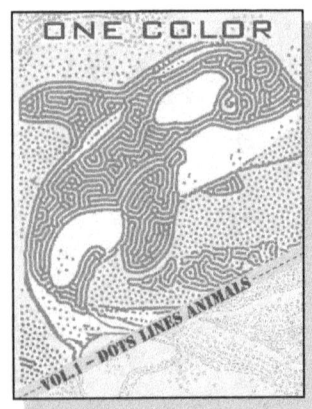 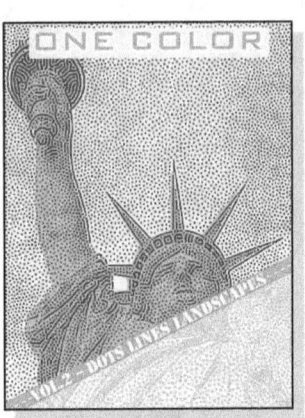 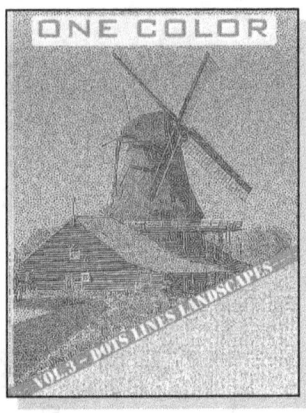 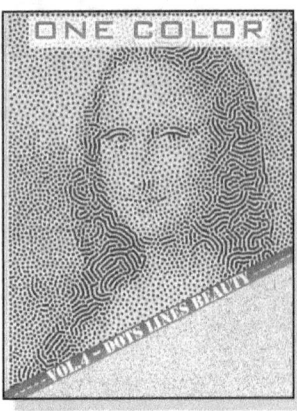

VOL. 1   VOL. 2   VOL. 3   VOL. 4

DOTS LINES SPIRAL

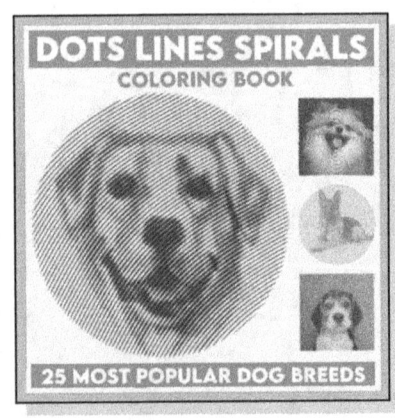 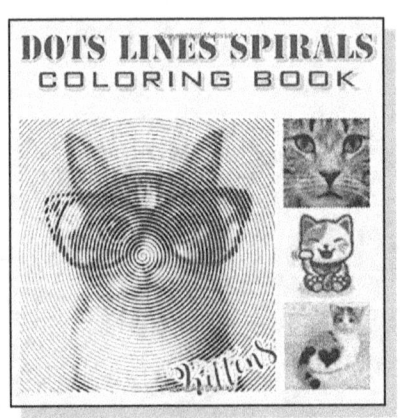 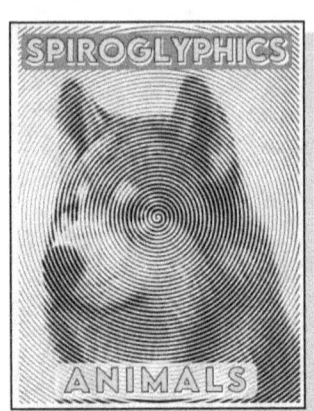

AND SO ON...

BRIGHT-IDEAS PAPER PUBLISHING
AMAZON.COM/AUTHOR/BRIGHT-IDEAS

Thank you for choosing Bright-Ideas Paper Publishing.
We hope you enjoy coloring your pages.

Feel free to share your colored pages with friends, family, and within the coloring community. Copying or otherwise reproducing uncolored pages is strictly forbidden.

A Special Request
LEAVE YOUR AMAZON REVIEWS

Show your support for us and help other colorists discover our artwork.

Simply find this book on Amazon, scroll to the reviews section, and click "Write a customer review"

Thank you for your purchases and reviews!

Copyright © 2020 Bright-Ideas Paper Publishing.
All Rights Reserved.

No part of this book may be reproduced or transmitted in any form or by any means, electronic or mechanical, including photocopying, recording or by any information storage and retrieval system, without written permission from the publisher.

The information provided within this book is for general informational purposes only. While we try to keep the information up-to-date and correct, there are no representations or warranties, express or implied, about the completeness, accuracy, reliability, suitability or availability with respect to the information, products, services, or related graphics contained in this book for any purpose.

Have a question or concern? Let us know
Bright-Ideas Paper Publishing | Bright.IdeasPaperPublishing@gmail.com

www.ingramcontent.com/pod-product-compliance
Lightning Source LLC
Chambersburg PA
CBHW081057240526
45465CB00025B/2462